Critical Condition:

Destructive Ideologies in America's Classrooms

by Matthew Nielsen

Contents

Introduction

"...schools exist for the education of children. Schools do not exist to provide iron-clad jobs for teachers, billions of dollars in union dues for teachers unions, monopolies for educational bureaucracies, a guaranteed market for teachers college degrees or a captive audience for indoctrinators."[1]

I was in second grade when my all-time favorite teacher, a Hispanic woman in her fifties, assigned the class to draw a self-portrait with crayons. I remember sitting at my desk coloring away when she came up beside me and asked about my drawing, "You're doing a great job on your drawing. Why are you using that color for your face?" I picked a color several shades darker than my actual skin tone and she noticed the discrepancy. "I don't know." She could see the look on my face and she knew me better than I knew myself at that age, I'm confident. "Try this one, instead" was her direction to me accompanied by a reassuring pat on the back and a smile. This is the only time I recall thinking about variations in skin tone during my younger years. My California elementary school was "majority minority," which made me—a decidedly Caucasian boy of mostly

---

[1] Sowell, T. (2020). *Charter schools and their enemies.* Basic Books. New York. (130).

Scandinavian descent—a minority. One afternoon, all of my classmates and I invited our parents to come to the school where we performed three traditional Mexican dances with our assigned partners. I had friends with every level of melanin imaginable— all of us lower-middle class. I have no doubt my perceptions on 'race' and 'race relations' are due, in significant part, to those formative years. It goes without saying that, today, critics would excoriate activities like this as cultural appropriation and, therefore, racist. No matter that the teacher who taught us the dances and arranged for our costumes, etc. was of Mexican heritage herself.

Still bad. Still wrong.

This is the world you and I live in.

'But, reasonable people don't actually believe any of those critiques, so what's the big deal? You're blowing it out of proportion.' Maybe. Not likely. The number of news instances detailing accounts of people that have every right to share their culture and heritage with their students, friends, or neighbors, is increasing.

Figure 1 | *Google search trendline for "Cultural appropriation"*
(from 2004-2021)

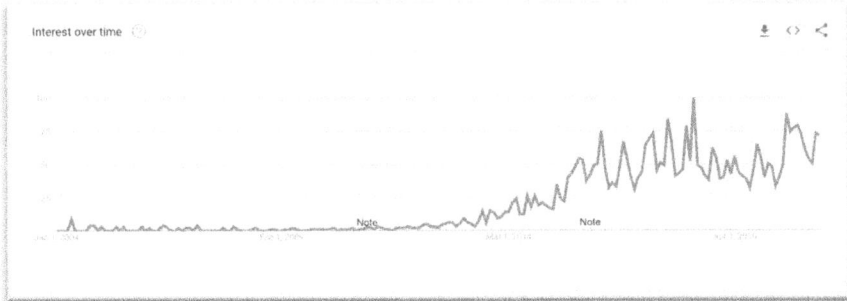

Interest over time

The outrage mob stands ready to pile on hapless commoners (you and I) who continue to interact normally with their friends of every background. It's simply no longer good enough. We must notice our differences along every dimension, discuss them, and apologize to one another for historic injustices that predate our relationships. I can't judge you based on how you've treated me personally. I need to know what people that look like you have done to harm people that look like me, which serves as the only accurate determinant of proper social relations, even at the interpersonal level. This idea removes personal responsibility from everyone and replaces it with deterministic essentialism. You can't help but perpetuate the oppression that your forebears imposed on other populations. Only the oppressed can free you (the oppressor)—along with themselves—from those damaging systems. So goes the argument.

The primary assertions of this argument rely completely on faith. Adherents of this ideology will only point to data, facts, and figures (very hesitantly) when absolutely required. And, when they do manage to identify a possible connection, it is tenuous at best (e.g. racism causes disproportionate incarceration rates, etc.) because they boil down—to a single variable—the complexity of unwieldy problems that have a host of causes (racism almost certainly is a factor in some cases of incarceration, but doesn't come close to explaining the totality of the issue). The requirement of faith for adherents of this ideology is evident in their reticence in providing proof of their claims. Moreover, when pressed, even the most ardent believers tend to either back off their hyperbole or resort to insults. As the great Dr. Thomas Sowell famously quipped, *"You can say that all you want, but the evidence is totally against you."*[2] The simple truth is that there is much more to the story than ideologues would have everyone believe.

I began writing this book on a Monday afternoon in February, 2021. For several years, I've been reading, watching, and listening to nearly everything I could get my hands on about Critical Theory, the Frankfurt School, Critical Race Theory, Postmodernism, and so on. The more I read, the more I seemed to notice the influence of these ideologies (pathologies?) in

---

[2] Sowell, T., Buckley, W.F., (1981, November 12). The Economic Lot of Minorities [TV series episode]. In *Firing Line with William F. Buckley*. Stanford University.

everyday life. Sometimes, I found it where it actually wasn't—a trap we all fall into from time to time. On this particular Monday, though, I read the latest news story in a long line of revelations about 7-year-olds being forced to deconstruct their identities in a public school classroom—by a teacher trained not in psychiatry, but in elementary education. I had read many very similar stories before that day and I've read many since. This Monday, though, I decided it was time to compile as much of these examples as I could and begin writing about why it may not be in anyone's best interest—anyone's, mind you—to make children do this.

This is not a book about 'race,' though it does address philosophies and ideologies that are concerned primarily with racism. Racism takes many forms, all of them reprehensible and antithetical to the ethics of the modern West. If readers take one thing away from this book, I hope it is this: Individuals should be free to make decisions for their own lives as long as they're not harming anyone else. In the context of education, this applies in this way: If a family wants their children to be educated in a school that is heavily influenced by Critical Theory or Postmodernism, they should have that opportunity. Similarly, if a family wants their children only to learn the basics of reading, writing, math, and science, they should be able to make that selection. To arrive at the place where this is possible, Americans—every American—need to be given the freedom to educate their children in the way they see fit. Instead of being forced to attend a government-run school you're assigned to simply as a function of your zip code, you should be able to select the school that will best meet the needs of your child. Average annual spending for students in grades K-12 is over $15,000 in the United States. Let families have that money to educate their children. Let them use it to pay for a private school, homeschool supplies, a charter school, or even for their local government-run school. We live in a pluralistic society that is fast becoming tribalistic. Polarization is leading friends and acquaintances to part ways because we're losing the ability to discuss important issues with one another. These fault lines are widening along distinctions between class, sexuality, and 'race.' And, there's no reason for it. Why are these the characteristics that are so important that they should define us and our ability to interact with other individuals? Who selected these, specifically? Should we all just accept that it's really the amount of melanin in our skin that should determine with whom we keep company, share a meal, or a conversation? This used to be called 'prejudiced,' and 'racist.' No longer is 'the content of our character' the ideal measurement, and it's a tragedy.

One particularly insidious form of racism, race essentialism, argues that because of the amount of melanin in your skin, society can automatically infer many of your characteristics: personality, preferences, and more. You are the way you are because of your complexion, or so goes the argument. This kind of thinking is so wrong it would be laughable if it weren't extremely damaging. Consider what this means in practice. If you have *more* melanin in your skin, your likes, dislikes, tendencies, and opportunities are objectively different than someone with *less* melanin. Is melanin that powerful? No, as it turns out. It's just not.

The problem would be big enough to warrant your attention if it was limited to adults. But, many parents aren't aware that their local school—their child's teacher—is including this in their reading, writing, history, science, and math lessons. Phrases like 'be yourself,' 'you're special,' and 'everyone is unique in their own way' are still used, but now there is a powerful tide pushing back against these ideas that advocates for 'the collective' over the individual. We see this in the way that groups of people are lumped together into categories, usually for political purposes. Wide swaths of people are bundled up and presented to the public (on the news, on social media, etc.) as a monolith: 'These people all believe and behave in the same ways, and how could it be otherwise? We know this because of their gender…their sex… their skin color, etc.

This flavor of identitarianism is harmful in absolute—not relative—terms, and it requires unflinching detachment from reality. Statistics, reason, logic, and even experience must be sacrificed to an identitarian ideology that has become so tightly woven into our culture, right under our noses. It's a rapidly growing cancer that discourages the individualistic ideals of the Enlightenment. Self-determination. Responsibility.

Accountability. Merit. Accomplishment. Each of these ideals, and many more, have been warped by the imposition of ideology.

Until a few years ago, if you were 'woke' you were aware of the unjust imbalances throughout society. An awareness of myriad examples of police brutality, in particular, has historically been a significant part of being 'woke.' Today, being woke means that you ignore reality and chase apparitions of oppression by leveraging actual disproportionalities; using exceptions to prove rules. There are large numbers of people in our society that are dispossessed. They struggle daily to get the very basics of life, even with safety nets in place via tax-supported welfare, etc. It is these realities—and the 'disparate impact' within them—that are dishonestly held up as proof-positive of 'systemic racism,' among other charges. Wokeness became a parody of its former self when every last connection to reality was severed.

The biggest purveyors of K-12 'wokeness' are undoubtedly the universities. Teacher colleges have been indoctrinating undergraduate students for decades now—a process that began as far back as 1970. The broader undergraduate and graduate populations in departments other than Education were on the receiving end of this for decades (to varying degrees) prior to the '70's, and particularly in the humanities. The result has been that college graduates of the last 50 years had at least a few Marxist professors; at least a few courses that advocated for a collectivist rather than individualist worldview; at least a few readings on Critical Theory, Postmodernism, and/or its variants.

You can think whatever you want. You would even be within your legal rights, in Western countries, to say nearly anything you want. We can thank the Enlightenment thinkers for freedom of speech[3]-- and, in part, for the idea that each individual should have rights and protections from harm by others. Increasingly, though, if the legal system won't punish you for thinking and saying things that some people don't like, society will.[4] We've been here before, of course. Social ostracism and banishment have been formally and informally imposed for millennia. The difference today is that we had a moment in time where nearly anything short of inciting violence was protected speech, even if it was deeply offensive. The controls on speech seem to be tightening—but directionally. In some Western countries, more stringent restrictions are already being codified in law. In others, the new restrictions are only socially enforced—for now. Regardless, both lead to similar outcomes: social shaming, loss of employment, and in some cases, loss of employability.[5] Not all ideas or comments are worth taking seriously, let alone

---

[3] Guider, A., (2015). *Freedom of expression and the Enlightenment.* University of Mississippi

[4] Spiked (2020). *25 times cancel culture was real.* Spiked Online. https://www.spiked-online.com/2020/07/14/25-times-cancel-culture-was-real/

[5] Gerstmann, E. (2020) *Cancel culture is only getting worse.* Forbes. https://www.forbes.com/sites/evangerstmann/2020/09/13/cancel-culture-is-only-getting-worse/?sh=3bdde65563f4

seriously considering. That goes without saying. As the old saying goes, however, 'sunlight is the best disinfectant.' If an increasing number of people don't feel comfortable sharing their views,[6] does this mean that the most extreme views simply disappear? Of course not. Without the disinfecting qualities of exposure to opposing views, those will almost certainly be reinforced and deepened.[7]

Who will fix the problem? You. You and your friends and neighbors. Even if you agree with many of the conclusions or policy prescriptions of the modern woke movement, the Machiavellian disregard for individual lives on the 'path of progress' is more than unsettling—it's anathema to a free society built on individual rights. This is no accident, of course. Wokeness in its current form is collectivistic, rather than individualistic. Whether believers know it or not, they're advocating for a society that values the collective more than the individuals within it—the opposite of Western civilization—by design. We need to be willing to stand up and speak out when we see things we know aren't right.

---

[6] Ekins, E., (2020). *Poll: 62% of Americans say they have political views they're afraid to share.* Cato Institute. https://www.cato.org/survey-reports/poll-62-americans-say-they-have-political-views-theyre-afraid-share

[7] Hedges, C. (2021) *Cancel culture: Where liberalism goes to die.* Scheer Post. https://scheerpost.com/2021/02/15/hedges-cancel-culture-where-liberalism-goes-to-die/

Part One will begin by discussing the significant changes that have helped to create today's education system. We'll then look at what Critical Theory is—along with its conceptual "cousins"—and how they became incorporated into math, English, science, and other lessons in classrooms throughout the United States.

In *Part Two*, we'll discuss how the circumstances of today's K-12 education system pose a problem for at least some students and families.

Finally, *Part Three* explores what can be done to solve the myriad problems that are posed by the destructive ideologies that are taught in America's classrooms.

Part 1: How Did We Get Here?

"...in each classroom somebody always does decide what material our children will be storing in their minds in the name of skills acquisition. All too often it is content for which our children will have no use in the future."[8]

During the past four centuries, the Western world has made unprecedented gains in science, technology, medicine, art, and more. It was during this period that Enlightenment thinkers turned civilization's focus to understanding the natural world, its wonders, and its possibilities. The myriad modern conveniences that we now enjoy are due in large part to their contributions to human knowledge. They, like us, had access to a long history of brilliant minds—from around the world—who contributed to advancements in math, philosophy, and other disciplines that created a foundation from which to build. The job remained, however, to piece together concepts and ideas, making new discoveries along the way that would ultimately make life more comfortable for everyone in different ways. This is their invaluable contribution to modern life. These same vital processes took place in the field of education.

---

[8] Hirsch, E.D., (1987). *Cultural literacy. What every American needs to know.* Vintage. New York. (144).

To observe an American 3rd grade classroom today is to witness the amalgamation of policies, practices, customs, and norms that were developed over the course of decades, centuries—even millennia. The idea that there is one teacher among many students hasn't always been the standard. Common curriculum (what should be taught in the classroom) between any number of schools (district, state, etc.) did not originate in America, though it certainly isn't a product of ancient Mesopotamia. Standardized curriculum is a concept that was developed between those two points in time, and while this is not a book focused on the history of education and its origins, a brief review of some of these important points in history is vital to understand why we find ourselves in our current situation.

Education history can be broadly categorized into three eras: pre-modern, modern, and postmodern.

Pre-modern Era (prior to 1500):

Authoritarian. Exclusive. Deterministic.

> Representative thoughts on education expressed by
> leading thinkers of the time:

44 B.C.: "…that right conduct is identical with expedient conduct and that no action whatsoever is expedient that is not also right conduct."[9]

ca. 1259: "…no created power can make something in a seminal state to become fully actual. Only God can do this. Therefore, humans cannot teach each other… The seeds of knowledge preexist in us… when the mind is helped by an outside power of reason. This is called teaching…"[10]

Modern Era (1500 to mid-1900s): Increasingly Egalitarian. Increasingly Inclusive. Indeterministic.

Representative thoughts on education expressed by leading thinkers of the time:

_1693_: "We naturally, as I said, even from our cradles, love liberty, and have therefore an aversion to many things, for no other reason, but because they are injoined us. I have always had a fancy, that

---

[9] Cicero, Marcus Tullius. (106 B.C. – 43 B.C.). (1887). _De officiis._ Cambridge. University Press.

[10] Aquinas, St. Thomas., (1225-1274) De veritate: De magistro. The Kolbe Foundation. http://www.kolbefoundation.org/gbookswebsite/studentlibrary/greatstbooks/aaabooks/aquinas/ontheteacher.html (Accessed 2021 March 2).

learning might be made a play and recreation to children."[11]

1748: "Obedience is so important that all education is actually nothing other than learning how to obey."[12]

Postmodern Era (mid-1900s to Present): Ideological. Schismatic. Relativistic.

Representative thoughts on education expressed by leading thinkers of the time:

1991: "[Postmodernism] does this by refusing forms of knowledge and pedagogy wrapped in the legitimizing discourse of the sacred and the priestly; its rejecting universal reason as a foundation for human affairs; claiming that all narratives are partial; and performing a critical reading on all scientific, cultural, and social texts as historical and political constructions."[13]

---

[11] Locke, John 1632-1704. (1996). *Some thoughts concerning education.* Hackett. (Cambridge, Massachussetts).

[12] Selzer, J.G., (1748). *Versuch von der erziehung und unterweisung der kinder (An essay on the education and instruction of children),* quoted in Alice Miller, *For Your Own Good* (New York). (2002), 8–14, http://www.nospank.net/fyog5.htm (accessed April 1, 2021).

[13] Giroux, H., (1991). *Postmodernism as border pedagogy: Redefining the boundaries of race and ethnicity* in *Postmodernism, feminism, and cultural politics: redrawing educational boundaries.* SUNY Press. New York.

1993: "It is meaningless to speak in the name of—or against—Reason, Truth, or Knowledge."[14]

Looking back over the development of education systems and practices, there are evident changes that range from subtle to revolutionary. Importantly, there was a large range of variation from one region or society to the next, even within the same time periods—as is the case today. For example, during the Hellenistic Period (323 B.C. to 33 B.C.), "As for the girls, from now on they went to primary and secondary schools just like the boys, and sometimes—and not only in Sparta—to the palestra and gymnasium."[15] This, of course, is more than can be said of some countries and regions, even in the 21st century—let alone during the same period. In the Persian Empire, the leaders of the Zoroastrian religion were responsible for the learning of the children.[16]

These three eras could easily be segmented further into shorter time periods to add specificity. But, for our purposes, pre-modern, modern, and post-modern will suffice. The developmental arc of education from ancient times to the present has tended toward inclusivity, empiricism, and specialization.

---

[14] May, T., (1993). *Between Genealogy and Epistemology: Psychology, Politics, and Knowledge in the Thought of Michel Foucault.* Pennsylvania State University Press. University Park, Pennsylvania.
[15] Marrou, H.I., (1982). *A history of education in antiquity.* University of Wisconsin Press. Madison. (103).
[16] Gibbons, E. (1776). *The decline and fall of the Roman empire.* Strahan & Cadell. London. 1(8).

During those thousands of years, there have most certainly been periods of restriction followed by expansion among various aspects of education. In terms of inclusivity, the past few hundred years have been largely characterized by expansion. Though not without blemish, that relatively recent history has produced largely positive results for students, families, and society as a whole. To pick up the history of education with sufficient context for where we are today, we need to discuss the genesis of the major constituent parts of America's education system as it currently exists. We'll then discuss four ideologies that are doing real damage in K-12 education today, along with how they're implemented practically in the classroom. The final chapter in Part One will review a specific and very popular concept that is reinforced among teachers and aspiring teachers throughout America, which encourages the politicization of K-12 students.

Chapter 1 | America's K-12 Education System

"The question is not, Does or doesn't public schooling create a public? The question is, What kind of public does it create? A conglomerate of self-indulgent consumers? Angry, soulless, directionless masses? Indifferent, confused citizens? Or a public imbued with confidence, a sense of purpose, a respect for learning, and tolerance? The right answer depends on two things, and two things alone: the existence of shared narratives and the capacity of such narratives to provide an inspired reason for schooling."[17]

Just as politics is downstream from culture, culture is downstream from education—and specifically, schools. The things we teach kids in elementary, middle, and high schools today will have a significant impact on what society looks like in 15-20 years from now, and beyond. This being the case, it's crucial that we place proper emphasis and priority on the education of children—if their learning wasn't reason enough by itself. The methods, approaches, and content are all important factors that should be carefully considered. Make no mistake about it, the status quo was born of plenty of arduous thought by very bright minds. And, regardless of whether everyone is happy

---

[17] Postman, N. (2011). The end of education. Redefining the value of school. Knopf Doubleday. New York. (18).

with the way it is, the current state of education today is the product of a long history.

A significant part of what we know today as the American education system finds its roots in 18th-century Prussia,[18] where Frederick the Great decreed (1763) that schooling would be **compulsory** and modeled on Johann Hecker's innovation of teaching students collectively rather than individually—something uncommon in German elementary education at the time.[19] Teaching in groups allowed for **standardization**. A consistently constructed and delivered education for children is appealing, at least to people in power. For government leaders with sufficient control over curriculum, a consistently trained citizenry makes an ideal pool of potential military or industrial personnel.

Like Prussia in the 1700s, American schooling today is compulsory, though there is some variance from state to state on the particulars.[20] In all 50 states, homeschooling is not only allowed, but it is considered a fulfillment of the compulsory requirement. The country's first compulsory attendance law was

---

[18] Dintersmith, T. (2015, October). Overturning the old model of education, *Boston Globe,* Opinion.

[19] Van Horn Melton, J. (1988). *Absolutism and the Eighteenth-Century Origins of Compulsory Schooling in Prussia and Austria.* Cambridge University Press.

[20] Katz, M.S., (1976). A History of Compulsory Education Laws. *Fastback Series, No. 75. Bicentennial Series.*

passed in the state of Massachusetts in 1852.[21] Horace Mann, among the most famous of early American education reformers, brought this novel approach to Massachusetts after a visit to Prussia where he observed the model in practice. The model was created to mold and shape youth into obedient citizens. Its originators "...sought to strengthen moral pillars of authority by refining its exercise. Central to this refinement was a shift in the technology of social discipline, whereby the locus of coercion was to be transferred from outside to inside the individual."[22]

Mann, himself, looked at the refinement and proper implementation of a public education system as a quasi-religious calling[23] that he was to fulfill. Religious overtones in expressions of commitment to duty, of course, were commonplace in the 19th century—and long before—since, outside of vocational training, formal education was born out of religion and religious tradition.[24] In Mann's own words, "I devote myself to the supremest [sic] welfare of mankind upon earth... I have faith in the improvability of the race, in their accelerating

---

[21] McDonald, K. (2017, September 6). Compulsory schooling is incompatible with freedom. Foundation for Economic Education. Retrieved on April 9, 2021: https://fee.org/articles/compulsory-schooling-is-incompatible-with-freedom/#:~:text=Horace%20Mann%2C%20the%20designer%20of,%2C%20but%20children%20are%20wax.%E2%80%9D

[22] Van Horn Melton, J. (1988). *Absolutism and the Eighteenth-Century Origins of Compulsory Schooling in Prussia and Austria.*

[23] Groen, M., (2008). *The Whig party and the rise of common schools, 1837-1854: party and policy reexamined.* American Educational History Journal, 35(2), 253.

[24] Fischer, S.R., (2004). *A History of Writing*, Reaktion Books, 36.

improvability... A spirit mildly devoting itself to a good cause is a certain conqueror... Here is a clew [sic] given by God to lead us through the labyrinth of the world."[25]

In short, if you can teach children from a young age to obey a defined set of rules that facilitate the goals of society's ruling class, there is much less need for coercion to achieve compliance in the service of those goals. In the Bible, this reads even more simply, "Train up a child in the way he should go, and when he is old, he will not depart from it."[26] And, in Mann's words, "Men are cast-iron, but children are wax."[27] We all know this to be the case, but wax in the hands of a demagogue is a very different thing from wax in the hands of loving parents.

The period from the 1890s through the 1930s was dominated by an intelligentsia who firmly believed that a modern utopia was attainable, if it was only managed properly[28], and that it required a variation on traditional Marxism (but tightly associated with it) and a race of people capable of ushering it in. Eugenics would take care of this last requirement.[29] This preoccupation with the pursuit of "the superior race" extended, predictably, into

---

[25] Mann, M.T.P., (1865). *Life and works of Horace Mann*, (80-81).
[26] Proverbs 22:6. King James Version (KJV).
[27] Mann, M.T.P., (1865). (13).
[28] Leonard, T.C. (2016). *Illiberal reformers. Race, eugenics, & American economics in the progressive era.* Princeton University Press. Princeton, New Jersey. (22).
[29] Ibid. (109).

education circles—in part, at least, through the country's largest teachers union (National Education Association):

"An erroneous conception of democracy and a faulty psychology have led a portion of the people of our country into an attempt to treat all men alike. The Indians must be given the white man's education, and social order, and transformed into white Indians. That the Indian is not a white man with a red skin has been learned at an enormous cost in dollars and a frightful waste of energy and life. When the Negro slaves were freed, they became, to some, white men with black skins, so that all that was needed to make them equal to the whites was to give them the white man's privileges and the white man's education. This attempt has likewise failed. The same faulty notions that led to an attempt to give the country child the same education as the city child, the tradesman's son the same as the son of his rich employer, the girls and women the same education as the boys and men, the illiterate adult the same as the child in the first grade. The failure of all these attempts, together with the teachings of modern psychology and sociology, has brought the whole country to accept the doctrine that differences do exist among men and that men should be treated accordingly."[30]

The official *Proceedings* of the union's annual meeting from 1910 indicates they had elected a representative to participate in the "Race Betterment Committee" (aka Race Betterment Foundation) that was founded in 1906 by Dr. John Harvey Kellogg—creator of Corn Flakes breakfast cereal.[31] Mrs. Susan

---

[30] Addresses and Proceedings - National Education Association of the United States. (1911). United States: (14).
[31] Kaelber, L. (n.d.). Michigan Eugenics. Retrieved on 2021 April 29: https://www.uvm.edu/~lkaelber/eugenics/MI/MI.html.

M. Dorsey of Los Angeles, California would be that representative for the NEA, and she would be taking the place of Adelaide S. Baylor.[32] Dorsey was the first female superintendent of Los Angeles City Schools, and Baylor was the first female superintendent of Wabash City Schools in Indiana. These educated, intelligent, and accomplished individuals allied themselves with an organization that was successful in assisting with the passage of Michigan's forced sterilization laws (1913).[33]

Professor A. F. Griffiths of Oahu University in Hawaii was a contributing editor of a research publication, *Journal of Race Development*, as well as a longtime member of the NEA. Professor Jeremiah W. Jenks is considered a founder of American economics—and also a eugenicist who provided trainings to NEA members. *Journal of Race Development* editor, G. Stanley Hall, was the president of Clark University in Worcester, Massachusetts in 1910 when the first volume of the journal was produced. Hall was appointed by Elmer Ellsworth Brown, then U.S. Commissioner of Education, as one of seven individuals to the International Council of Education. This council was the brainchild of the NEA during its 1910 annual meeting.[34]

---

[32] Addresses and Proceedings - National Education Association of the United States. (1910). United States: (109).
[33] Kaelber, L. (n.d.).
[34] Volume Information. (1910). *The Journal of Race Development, 1*(1). Retrieved April 29, 2021, from http://www.jstor.org/stable/29737841

Clearly, eugenics was a favorite pseudoscience of the intelligentsia during that period. The who's who of K-12 education were intimately involved in some of the most overtly racist and discriminatory clubs, committees, and policies of the 20th century—which is saying something. It is no wonder that in the decades following this period laws and enforcement of those laws perpetuated this quasi-religious pseudoscience—even if not explicitly. To what extent do these ideas continue to flavor the philosophies of the 'education establishment,' If they do at all? Is it possible that these ideas never truly went away—that they were simply incorporated piecemeal into a transforming philosophy of education? Echoes of the belief in race-differentiated intellectual capacity are certainly evident in today's U.S. education policy and university departments of education. The inculcation of all children—via compulsory attendance laws—at the hands of teachers operating within this system may be seen as the natural result of removing parental power from the education of their children. Removing from parents the power to choose what is best for children has very often resulted in outcomes that are anything but 'the best.'

Three hundred years ago, a child's education was most often solely in the hands of their parents. For the wealthy, private in-home tutors or boarding schools were the norm in the late 1700s. The poor kids had to settle for group settings with standardized curriculum. Not much has changed in this regard. Today, parents with resources may still opt for boarding schools or tutors, but might also send their children to an elite private school or even a high-performing government-run school. Typically, the highest-performing district schools tend to be surrounded by neighborhoods where homes are very expensive. Most states' education funding models perpetuate this system by supplying schools with a portion of property taxes from nearby homeowners. What does this mean for schools located in areas where homes have lower assessed values? Less funding. Parents with adequate resources who want the best education for their children at a district school, pay what is often referred to as 'tuition via mortgage.'[35] This is the most common form of school choice in America. Because this has been common practice for so long, most people are blind to its reality. Many otherwise caring and generous people don't see any problem with their opposition to school choice measures (like charter schools, education savings accounts, or even homeschooling) that would afford underprivileged students opportunities to select the educational option that best meets their needs—while they, with plenty of financial means, buy into the best local schools by moving into a pricey neighborhood. The uniqueness of each child is evident to parents—and anyone else that's ever paid attention. A standardized approach to over 50 million unique individuals—what has been called 'a one-size-fits-all model of

---

[35] Shuls, J. (2012, April 10). *School choice by mortgage*. Show Me Institute. Retrieved on April 9, 2021: https://showmeinstitute.org/blog/school-choice/school-choice-by-mortgage

education—is simply bad policy. It also happens to be ignorant, and sometimes hypocritical. That is, unless the goal is simply to create and maintain an obedient populace.

For everyone that can't afford the pricey mortgage or private school tuition, taxpayer-funded education is the default. Where available, charter schools provide tuition-free alternatives to district schools—and there are over 7,000 charter schools operating in the United States today. Interestingly, some of the highest-performing charter schools in the country serve some of the most underprivileged students.[36] Charter schools, private schools, and homeschooling options very often operate outside the norms of the standardized government schools. There is much less regulation imposed on private schools and homeschoolers than on government schools. Charter schools are typically regulated less than government schools, but more than private and home schools. This break from the standardization that the Prussians and Horace Mann so desired for others is rapidly growing in popularity,[37] and for good reason. The uniqueness of individuals demands a variety of educational options to meet their needs. Where viable options are made

[36] Sowell, T. (2020). Charter schools and their enemies. Basic Books. New York.

[37] AFC. (2021, April 6). *Real clear opinion research poll: School choice support soars.* American Federation for Children. Retrieved on April 10, 2021: https://www.federationforchildren.org/real-clear-opinion-research-poll-school-choice-support-soars/

available to families, they're often quickly filled to capacity and then wait-listed.

American children today are taught in groups (collectively) rather than individually, again mirroring the Prussian system. Another late-1700's innovation of Hecker's is very familiar to Americans today—raising one's hand before speaking. Borrowing and adopting these characteristics, among others, required a transplant of the system from Prussia to America. This transplant was performed by public education advocate and politician Horace Mann in the 1850's, as mentioned previously.

American children today grow up in a vastly different educational reality than the laissez faire approach of the 17th, 18th, and 19th' centuries. Of course, not all children were afforded the same opportunities for learning during this time. As it was illegal to educate any enslaved person prior to 1865, it goes without saying that the evils of the institution of slavery extended far beyond the immorality of stealing another human's freedom and labor. To forcibly limit another person's education for the purpose of retaining control over them is no less depraved than robbing them of their physical freedom. There's likely a convincing argument that it is more detrimental, in fact, to deprive a person of learning—and so to limit their learning—than it is to limit their physical freedom, to come and go as they please. Both physical and intellectual freedom require a commitment to and belief in the capacity of every human being to learn and grow. We build facilities and organizations to make these opportunities for growth available to children, and we spend a lot of money doing it. But, there is a glaring disconnect between our stated goals, the ones we proclaim in public, and where we spend education dollars. This is a problem that has been well-documented and, simultaneously, dismissed as unimportant and misrepresented. During a span of about 50 years, per-pupil education spending in the United States increased by 280% in real terms. Over that same time period, spending on administrative, non-teaching staff and non-instructional expenses increased by over 1862% while teacher pay has only increased 17% in real terms. Student achievement hasn't kept pace with that spending, suggesting that maybe money isn't always the answer. Add to this the fact that when kids are given a choice of where to attend school they tend to get better grades, and the case for more choice and less spending becomes even more convincing.

We've arrived at a place in education's history where, for many people, the institution is more important than the outcomes it produces, or even the content that it teaches. Of course, we've got our priorities wrong, so long as we all continue to act as if children are made for schools and not the other way around. To reach this commonsense conclusion, however, we have to use reason and logic, both of which are losing ground to Critical Theories and their various 'sub-species' and Postmodernism in universities, colleges, K-12 schools, and even preschools. The following chapters in Part One will answer these four questions about several of these theories: 'What is it?' 'Where did it come from?' 'Where can it be found?', and 'Who are its advocates and critics?'

Chapter 2 | The 1970's & Critical Race Theory

"...people are more readily oppressed when they are already perceived as inferior by nature. The reverse is more to the point. People are more readily perceived as inferior by nature when they are already seen as oppressed."[38]

What is it?

Everything in our world is power, the distribution of which is mediated by race (e.g. broad categorizations of Asian, Black, Caucasian, Hispanic, Native, Pacific Islander, etc.).[39] Every human construction, from governments to homeschool co-ops are embedded in racial structures that fundamentally build or dismantle racism and white supremacy. All people, regardless of socioeconomic status, location, or personality cannot help but perpetuate or undermine systems of racial oppression. This is Critical Race Theory in a nutshell.

For adherents of this theory, Martin Luther King, Jr's dream is idealistic nonsense. The only path of progress is through the

---

[38] Fields, K., Fields, B. (2014). *Racecraft. The soul of inequality in American life.* Verso. Brooklyn, New York. (128).

[39] Biologists do not use the term "race" to differentiate between people with variations in melanin levels. Race is a purely cultural and rhetorical phenomenon, which has no basis in biology.

rubble of a completely dismantled America. Why? Critical Race Theory (CRT) asserts that the very structure of society is systemically oppressive to minority populations, and that racism is built into the very fabric of social life. So much so, that even when overtly racist policies, practices, or actions are 'removed' or 'rectified,' racism is still present—it is simply manifesting in new ways.[40]

As a result, racism cannot ever truly be solved, according to CRT. This belief creates a truly dangerous situation. Children are being taught that they live in a society that is riddled with racism and hate. They are being told that, due to factors outside their control—their melanin levels—they are oppressed, or they are the oppressors. They are also being taught that there is no resolution to this problem.

> *"There are five major components or tenets of CRT: (1) the notion that racism is ordinary and not aberrational; (2) the idea of an interest convergence; (3) the social construction of race; (4) the idea of storytelling and counter-storytelling; and (5) the notion that whites have actually been recipients of civil rights legislation."*[41]

---

[40] Delgado, R., Stefancic, J. (1998). Critical Race Theory: Past, Present, and Future, *Current Legal Problems*, 51(1), 467–491, https://doi.org/10.1093/clp/51.1.467

[41] Hartlep, N.D. (2009). *Critical race theory: An examination of its past, present, and future implications.* University of Wisconsin at Milwaukee. Retrieved on 2021 May 13: https://files.eric.ed.gov/fulltext/ED506735.pdf.

Consider what havoc this is likely to wreak on young minds. "We have a problem. You are the problem, and there is no way to fix it. You'll never be able to do enough to repair the damage that you perpetuate simply by existing." CRT is incredibly disempowering. Children who are placed in the 'oppressed' category are told that the system is rigged against them. In such a situation, why should a child make any attempt to succeed?

This is the kind of cult-like ideology that encourages people to call for the extermination of "all white people." As you can see, "white people just don't like being on the defensive" is an insufficient response to the vastly understated charge that Critical Race Theory falls short of usefulness or even coherence. CRT is an ideology that has justified the repudiation of principles of equality espoused by Dr. Martin Luther King, Jr.

> *"Unlike traditional civil rights, which stresses incrementalism and step-by-step progress, critical race theory questions the very foundations of the liberal order, including equality theory, legal reasoning, Enlightenment rationalism, and neutral principles of constitutional law."[42]*

CRT calls for the demonization of people based solely on their melanin levels. So, in response to a universally-recognized gross

---

[42] Delgado, R., Stefancic, J. (1995). Critical race theory: An introduction. NYU Press. New York. (3).

injustice that spanned centuries—from slavery and murder to segregation and false imprisonment—activists and demagogues now advocate for more of the same, but in the other direction. This continuation of racism, in the name of social justice—what we'll refer to as neo-racism—is in response to historical harms, but among people today who were neither victims nor perpetrators of those horrific, and recognized, evils. Those demagogues who promote this go so far as to include 'objectivity' and 'promptness' as characteristics of white supremacy culture.

Like many academic ideas, Critical Race Theory was simply a recycling and grafting of an older set of ideas that took shape over 40 years before Bell and Delgado first started publishing their related works. Their ideas are most closely related to Critical Theory—the philosophy from which it gained its name and its fundamental approach to understanding and explaining the world. We'll discuss Critical Theory in the next chapter.

CRT is unfalsifiable and essentialist.[43] The fact that it is unfalsifiable, taken alone, makes it a strong candidate for classification as a religious sect[44] or cult, rather than simply a theory.

---

[43] Pluckrose, H., Lindsay, J. (2020). *Cynical theories.* Pitchstone. Durham, North Carolina. (111-134).

[44] McWhorter, J. (2018 April 14). Antiracism, our flawed new religion. The Daily Beast. Retrieved on 2021 May 15: https://www.thedailybeast.com/antiracism-our-flawed-new-religion.

Where did it come from?

The founding theorists of CRT, Derrick Bell (1930-2011) and Richard Delgado (b. 1939), began formulating these ideas specifically in a legal context (Critical Legal Theory). In that context, the central position of the theory is that one's race determines the outcomes of legal proceedings, necessarily, because the laws themselves are racist (meant to effectuate disparate impacts on minorities). The classist and racist practice of redlining was (justifiably) targeted for critique as well. Some of these practices continue today—albeit under new and extremely misleading names like 'opportunity zones.' That these practices were and are carried out in cities around the United States, while not widely known or understood, is nonetheless impossible to dispute. Critical Race Theorists take up problems like redlining, which indisputably need solving, and attach a litany of spurious accusations as explanations of the causes. The baggage that comes with CRT has led many to reject the veracity of verifiable real-world problems—a development that turns away potential supporters who are simply turned off by hyperbole. Proponents are not doing themselves any favors by insisting that all problems are the result of white supremacy at their root and that the proper framework through which to view the world is Marxism (oppressor vs. oppressed).

The rhetorical tools they used, then and now, were quickly applied to other fields of study, including education:

Today, many scholars in the field of education consider themselves critical race theorists who use CRT's ideas to understand issues of school discipline and hierarchy, tracking, affirmative action, high-stakes testing, controversies over curriculum and history, bilingual and multicultural education, and alternative and charter schools.[45]

Whether a function of taste or practicality, critical theorists have consistently rejected the use of logic and reason (hence 'rhetorical tools' and not 'logical tools'). Because both of these are primary examples of White Hegemony[46], they, themselves, are tools of oppression.[47]

This rejection of logic and reason has prompted some critics to say what many are already thinking: *"...garbled, pretentious writing is recast as possessing a genius above clarity..."*[48] But, pretentious as it may be, it holds real currency in society: *"Fifty years ago, it was a source of shame to be the first person to cry*

---

[45] Delgado, R., Stefancic, J., (1995). *Critical race theory: An introduction.* NYU Press. (New York).

[46] Hegemony (n): leadership or dominance, especially by one country or social group over others. *Oxford Languages*

[47] White supremacy culture. (n.d.) Dismantling Racism. Retrieved April 2, 2021 from https://www.dismantlingracism.org/white-supremacy-culture.html

[48] Zorn, J. (2018). Critical Race Theory in Education: Where Farce Meets Tragedy. *Academic Questions, 31*(2), 203+. https://link.gale.com/apps/doc/A538294128/AONE?u=maricopa_main&sid=AONE&xid=eae0fce6

"Uncle"; you were a loser. Today, you win. In the new environment, "I hurt" establishes rights."[49]

Bell, "…whose work is either praised in public or dismissed as mediocre in private…"[50] became the public face of CRT while the workload for production of 'scholarship' and 'research' on the topic was much more broadly distributed, and increasingly so as time passed. Interestingly, one of the big problems that CRT claims to want to fix is the "centering of whiteness." But, in the ongoing effort to rid society of this alleged scourge, "whiteness" is very often at the center of the conversation; a paradox worth noting, but not out of line with a dismissal of logic. It started out as a vehicle to prominence for mediocre academics. Now people actually take it seriously. That's a problem. To the extent that anything positive could have come from Bell and Delgado's writings, it would have to be a recognition that disparate impact is real. They missed the mark on where the proper locus of measurement for that impact should be taken, however. Because every individual is unique, policies affect everyone—everyone—differently. The smallest minority is the individual. For this reason, it is improper to create policies or programs based solely on the ethnicity or melanin levels of groups of people.[51]

---

[49] Subotnik, D. (2005). Toxic diversity: Race, gender, and law talk in America. NYU Press. New York. (62).

[50] Crouch, S. (1995). *The all-American skin game, or the decoy of race.* Pantheon. New York. (75).

[51] Abrams, S. J. (2021, March 23). *Data prove people self-censor in fear of woke mobs.* Real Clear Policy. Retrieved on 2021 April 24:

Individual liberty and "neutral principles of constitutional law" are exactly what should be pursued.

Where can it be found?

Critical Race Theory can be found in universities and colleges[52], high schools[53], middle schools/junior high schools[54], elementary schools[55], and even preschools[56]—yes, preschools. Teacher colleges throughout the country are filled with "...these scholars [who] tend to think race permeates and defines every aspect of schooling."[57]

---

https://www.realclearpolicy.com/articles/2021/03/23/data_prove_peo
ple_self-censor_in_fear_of_woke_mobs_769331.html

[52] Hess, R., Burke, L., (2021, April 5). *Does race get short shrift in education research and teacher training?* American Enterprise Institute. Heritage Institute. https://www.heritage.org/education/report/does-race-get-short-shrift-education-research-and-teacher-training

[53] Rickert, O., (2018, April 13). *Student: What white privilege lessons did to my high school.* Intellectual Takeout. Retrieved on 2021, April 5: https://www.intellectualtakeout.org/article/student-what-white-privilege-lessons-did-my-high-school/

[54] NASP. (n.d.) Talking about race and privilege: Lesson plan for middle and high school students. National Association of School Psychologists. Accessed April 5, 2021. https://www.nasponline.org/resources-and-publications/resources-and-podcasts/diversity-and-social-justice/social-justice/social-justice-lesson-plans/talking-about-race-and-privilege-lesson-plan-for-middle-and-high-school-students

[55] Schwartz, K., (2019, September 17). Teaching 6-year-olds about privilege and power. KQED. Accessed April 5, 2021. https://www.kqed.org/mindshift/54150/teaching-6-year-olds-about-privilege-and-power

[56] Brown, M., (2020, August 5). How to explain white privilege in terms simple enough for a child. *Parents.* https://www.parents.com/kids/responsibility/racism/how-to-explain-white-privilege-in-term-simple-enough-for-a-child/

[57] Hess, R., Burke, L. (2021).

The most popular curriculum that uses a CRT framework, having made national headlines over the past few years, is the 1619 Project.

This curriculum has been adopted at several school districts58 in the United States and is an outgrowth of a series of articles59 that began in the New York Times under the direction of journalist Nikole Hannah-Jones. Lawmakers in three states, at the time of this writing, have introduced legislation that would ban the use of this curriculum in any public schools.60 An organization called WhatAreTheyLearning.com aggregates news stories about 'woke curriculum' and trainings in districts schools in the United States on their website. After spending a few minutes on their site and reading about what is going on around the country, it quickly becomes clear that this is a growing trend.

---

[58] Riley, N.S., (2020). The 1619 project enters American classrooms. Education Next. Accessed April 5, 2021: https://www.educationnext.org/1619-project-enters-american-classrooms-adding-new-sizzle-slavery-significant-cost/

[59] Hannah-Jones, N., (n.d.). 1619 Project. New York Times. Accessed April 5, 2021: https://www.nytimes.com/interactive/2019/08/14/magazine/1619-america-slavery.html

[60] Schwartz, S. (2021, February 3). Lawmakers push to ban '1619 project' from schools. Education Week. Accessed April 5, 2021: https://www.edweek.org/teaching-learning/lawmakers-push-to-ban-1619-project-from-schools/2021/02

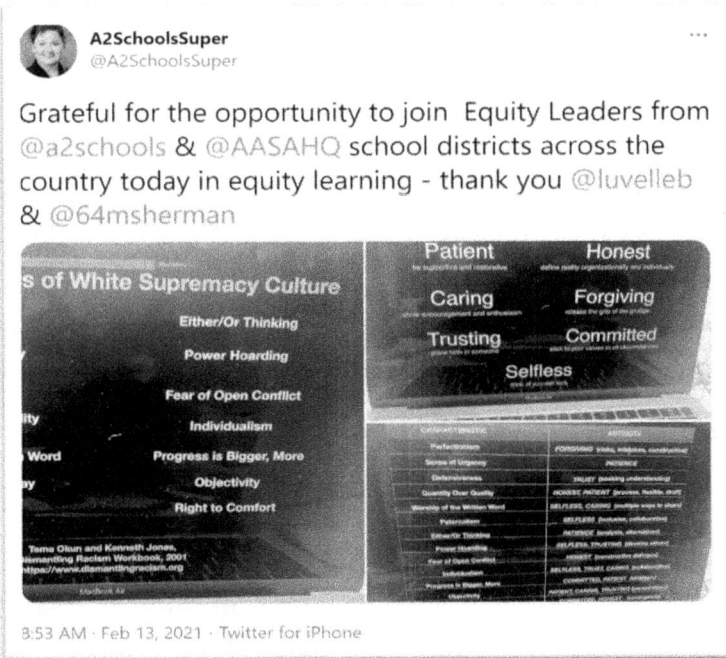

A2SchoolsSuper
@A2SchoolsSuper

Grateful for the opportunity to join Equity Leaders from @a2schools & @AASAHQ school districts across the country today in equity learning - thank you @luvelleb & @64msherman

8:53 AM · Feb 13, 2021 · Twitter for iPhone

So, it's being taught in K-12 district schools, what about private schools?

Of course, these ideas already feature prominently in urban and suburban areas. But, don't think your kids won't be taught these things because you live in a rural area, or a 'more conservative' area. The likelihood is that they will. Does your child attend a religious school? There, too, they will learn this.[61]

---

[61] Sacred Heart Education. (n.d.). Sacred heart education. Fighting systemic racism. Accessed April 5, 2021:
https://www.sacredheartusc.education/fighting-systemic-racism

Who are its advocates and critics?

Dr. Ibram Xolani Kendi (born Ibram Henry Rogers) is an influential academic, speaker, and author of 'How to be an Anti-Racist.' Kendi's parents were both working professionals during his youth, his mother a healthcare business analyst and his father a tax accountant. He completed undergraduate work in African American Studies and magazine production at Florida A&M University. He received a PhD in African American Studies from Temple University in 2010. His work repeatedly asserts that one can only be racist or anti-racist—there is no such thing as 'not racist.'[62] It has been asserted that 'either/or thinking' reinforces white supremacy. Kendi's insistence that you're either racist or antiracist, of course, is an exception to this rule.

Robin DeAngelo famously wrote and published her 2018 book, *White Fragility*, which has been praised and ridiculed. The central message of the book is that white people avoid talking about race because it makes them feel uncomfortable—so uncomfortable that they'll go so far as to deny the existence of racism completely. If you admit you're a white racist, you're

---

[62] @DrIbram. (2020, May 26). I keep saying there's no such thing as being "not racist." We are either being racist or antiracist. And in order to be antiracist, we must, first and foremost, be willing to admit the times we are being racist, which #AmyCooper failed to do, which many Amy Coopers fail to do. [Tweet] Retrieved from https://twitter.com/DrIbram/status/1265300114849087488?s=20

helping society to heal. If you don't admit it, you're simply a liar and you're perpetuating white supremacy.

Critics of CRT often cite the illogical and deterministic essentialism of the ideology as a glaring deficiency. In their very thorough and thought-provoking book, *Racecraft*, sisters Karen and Barbara Fields systematically dismantle the idea of race itself—leaving CRT enthusiasts in a quandary, "how can critical *race* theory be valid if race isn't what we think it is?" And, it isn't—if you believe biologists. *"...the assignment of black Americans to slavery did not follow automatically from their color or ancestry."*[63] Advocates are quick to point out that CRT is explicitly anti-essentialist. This is true, but only in the rhetorical sense.[64] With some simple internet searches anyone can find direct quotes from the leading Theorists denouncing race-essentialism. However, it becomes impossible to square those claims with other stated positions and practice. From one side of the advocate's mouth we hear, "CRT rejects race-essentialism." From the other side we hear, "The mere existence of white people perpetuates oppression of minority groups,"[65] and "People of color exist in an inescapably racist society where success isn't possible simply because of the color of their skin.

[63] Fields, K., Fields, B., (2014). (110).

[64] K., M. (2020 June 6). *Yes, my dear, all white people are racists.* Age of Awareness. Retrieved on 2021 May 5: https://medium.com/age-of-awareness/yes-all-white-people-are-racist-eefa97cc5605.

[65] Carmack, E. (2015 February 26). *Dear white people.* The Campanil. Retrieved on 2021 May 5: http://www.thecampanil.com/dear-white-people-how-to-combat-racism/.

Even if one of them manages to become financially successful, they are simply being oppressed in new ways that may not be easily perceived."

Stanley Crouch (1945-2020), poet, musician, author, and jazz critic, repeatedly penned counterpoints to the early proponents of Critical Race Theory: *"I accuse [Derrick] Bell and his ilk of being, fundamentally, defeatists, people who accept high positions of success, then tell those below them that they don't have a chance."*[66] Crouch was on a discussion panel (1993) with Derrick Bell and other "dinosaur dragons from the sixties," from which he recalls correcting Bell on the point that nothing had ever benefitted black Americans that wasn't the result of white Americans acting in their own interest. Bell conceded that he had "overstated the case."[67] We're left to wonder how often he and his comrades have exaggerated over the course of decades with their hyperbole going unchecked. Crouch was willing to speak up and question Bell's claim in the moment, causing Bell to back down and admit to getting carried away. 'Maybe those exaggerations continue today' …sure. Let's say 'maybe' to leave some wiggle room for error. There's really no reason to believe even for a moment, because there are so few people who have been willing to question CRT's claims, that 'overstating the case' is anything less than commonplace among proponents.

---

[66] Crouch, S. (1995). (76).
[67] Ibid.

As CRT has gained traction in various academic disciplines, its precepts have oozed out into the wider societal conversation and culture where they are occasionally questioned and rebutted. But, there are still a few academics taking advocates to task all the way back at Derrick Bell's Critical Legal Studies. For instance, Touro University professor Dan Subotnik wrote a book on the topic, where he asks and answers a long list of questions, among them: "So, is it anti-black conspiracies that are keeping African Americans down, as race theorists maintain? Or is it antiblack-conspiracy theorizing that is doing so?"[68]

The infection rate of CRT among Western institutions over the past 50 years has been nothing short of epidemic. Why do so many otherwise intelligent people take up and evangelize for these ideas? As Jeff Zorn notes, "...*sweet benefits kick in: niches abound for teaching, lecturing, and publishing;*"[69] Recent history has shown us how lucrative such an enterprise can be, but we're left to wonder, along with Glenn Loury, "...how did the children profit?"[70]

It would be wrong not to mention the work of Walter Williams, John McWhorter, Coleman Hughes, Chloe Valdary, K'mele Foster, Thomas Chatterton Williams, and, here, Shelby Steele: "The great evil of America's oppression of blacks was the use of

---

[68] Subotnik, D. (2005). (107).
[69] *Zorn, J., (2018).*
[70] Loury, G. quoted in Woodson, R. (1987). On the road to economic freedom. An agenda for black progress. Regnery Gateway. New York. (117).

the collective quality of color to limit us as individuals no matter our talents or energies—individual autonomy stifled by oppressive collectivism."[71] That collectivism[72] continues now under the guise of "progress" through CRT. All of these individuals, and many more unnamed, have contributed significantly to exposing the ills of CRT as well as offering better alternatives.

Steele goes on to say, "…racial development will always be the effect that results from individuals within the race bettering their own lives."[73] CRT downplays the efficacy and value of personal effort and merit.

---

[71] Steele, S. (1990). *The content of our character. A new vision of race in America.* St. Martin's Press. New York. 159.

[72] Hicks, S.R.C. (2004). (158).

[73] Steele, S. (1990). *The content of our character. A new vision of race in America.* St. Martin's Press. New York. 159.

Chapter 3 | The 1930's & Critical Theory

"Individuals are not in control of their feelings: their identities are a product of their group memberships, whether economic, sexual, or racial. Since the shaping economic, sexual, or racial experiences or developments vary from group to group, differing groups have no common experiential framework. With no objective standard by which to mediate their different perspectives and feelings, and with no appeal to reason possible, group balkanization and conflict must necessarily result."[74]

What is it?

Everything in our world is power. Systems and structures are created to maintain and build upon that power. Everyone is either oppressed or an oppressor. One must ruthlessly critique everything in existence. Scientific rationality is pernicious. Critical Theory is "...*practical* in a distinctively moral (rather than instrumental) sense."[75] In other words, "critical" arguments are formed and founded in rhetoric—only. As a result, one

---

[74] Hicks, S.R.C. (2004). (82).
[75] Stanford University (2010). *Critical Theory.* Stanford Encyclopedia of
        Philosophy, Stanford University.
        https://plato.stanford.edu/entries/critical-theory/

cannot test their claims with any instrument of measurement. This is Critical Theory in a nutshell.

So, if you can't test its claims, how can anyone know whether its claims are true or not? This requires faith or 'suspension of disbelief,' whichever you prefer. Seriously, though, without an option to test claims, the only choices available are (1) to believe, (2) not care enough to consider the claims either way, or (3) disbelieve. There is a serious question that can and should be asked at this point: Is it reasonable or accurate to call this a 'theory' given that it is unfalsifiable? Granted, Critical Theory offers a 'set of tools that helps to explain and interpret the world and life experiences.' But, without changing the definition of the word 'theory,' it seems ill-suited for such a name.

It is intentionally subjective—everyone on the planet can come up with a different conclusion given a standardized set of inputs and this 'theory' would not be proven wrong, and such an outcome would not be suspicious in the least. This is what one would expect, considering its solipsistic relativism. The old saying, 'perception is reality' is taken literally and all-inclusively. Without the ability to falsify the assertions of Critical Theory-so called, and its many offspring (Critical Race Theory, Critical Gender Theory, Critical Pedagogy, etc.), each of these are actually better categorized as ideologies, cults, or religions.

What value does Critical Theory really have to anyone? So far, it's been a very effective method of creating additional faculty jobs at universities. And, because it accepts and perpetuates the oppressor/oppressed worldview, it has the added benefit of creating for its proponents social protections that are granted to 'allies of the oppressed.' Why does it focus on morals, and who decides what is moral and what is not? This is a subjective question that is dependent on time and place—due to historical materialism. But, a moral system must preserve protections for the proletariat and repel oppression. Capitalism is immoral because it alienates and reifies individuals. A moral system is one that liberates the individual. So argue the 'crits.'

Critical Theory, like the Western Marxism from which it sprang, is primarily concerned with the emancipation of the individual from oppressive structures.[76] As historical materialists, they believed that matter, material, systems, and structures created reality—as opposed to humans creating reality through their own consciousness and ideals. The path of history is always determined by systems, not ideals. For the later critical theorists, any dominant societal structure (or hegemony) is oppressive because it imposes on individuality.

Confused yet? We're only getting started.

---

[76] Bronner, S.E. (2017). *Critical Theory*. Oxford University Press. New York. 18.

Where did it come from?

Goethe University Frankfurt, like several other German institutions, was one of the preeminent universities leading up to and during the interwar period of the early 1900s. Few American universities granted doctoral degrees until the early 1900s, and still fewer had graduate programs that held any credibility internationally.[77] This meant that many individuals who wanted to pursue a career in academia went to Europe to gain the necessary credentials. During this time, the *Institute for Social Research* was created by Friedrich Pollock and Felix Weil with a professor of political law and economy at University of Vienna named Carl Grunberg installed as its first director. The *Institute* was bankrolled by Weil, a wealthy student at Frankfurt. All of them were neo-Marxists. Critical Theory took the Marxian 'oppressor/oppressed' framework and began to apply it to a field outside of markets and economics[78]—an approach they hoped would help explain the failures of Marx's economic prescriptions—social psychology.[79]

---

[77] Thurgood, L., Golladay, M.J., Hill, S.T. (2006). *U.S. Doctorates in the 20th Century.* National Science Foundation. Retrieved on 2021 May 25: https://wayback.archive-it.org/5902/20160210153510/http://www.nsf.gov/statistics/nsf06319/ .

[78] Leonard, T. C. (22).

[79] Hicks, S.R.C., (2004). *Explaining postmodernism: Skepticism and socialism from Rousseau to Foucault.* Ockham's Razor.

While they generally agreed with Marx, they felt many gaps were left in his writings that required development and explanation. The *Institute* (now commonly referred to as *The Frankfurt School*) was formed with the vision of filling in those conceptual gaps through the work of its members. Most notably, these scholars argued, in effect, "Not only was the Social Democratic leadership too wishy-washy and compromising, its voting constituencies among the working classes were themselves clueless about their real needs and their real but masked state of oppression."[80] A strong commitment to Marx pushed the Critical Theorists to deeply question the inability of such a desirable and potent philosophy (communism) to motivate the proletariat to rise up in revolution. The oppressed, they reasoned, were either lazy or blind. They concluded that they would need more levers to pull—more points of access to the minds of the masses—to wake up the workers of the world to their oppression. It became obvious to members of the *Institute* that the workers needed leadership. The leading lights of *The Frankfurt School* had agreed that what the Marxists really needed was an aristocracy—a role they could fill. The major result of this work is what is now known as Critical Theory.

Some of the Frankfurt School's more recognizable names include Horkheimer, Marcuse, and Adorno. Of course, they each

---

[80] Hicks, S.R.C., (2004). *Explaining postmodernism: Skepticism and socialism from Rousseau to Foucault.* Ockham's Razor. 140.

differed from one another on particular points of their ideology, but the fundamental theoretical underpinnings—noted above—of the *School* were largely undisputed among members of the group.

Max Horkheimer—who was involved with the *Institute* from the beginning—pursued his doctoral studies under Hans Cornelius, a neo-Kantian philosopher, at Frankfurt. Horkheimer was a major influence on *The Frankfurt School*, becoming its second director after the departure of Grunberg due to illness. Both Grunberg and Horkheimer were skeptical of epistemology and reason. They fostered that skepticism among others through their writings and speaking events. While they nurtured doubts about shared reality and objectivity, they pursued Kant's anti-Enlightenment ideas that prioritized subjectivity and emotion.

This importation of Marxist critiques to a field outside socio-economic structures is what makes *The Frankfurt School* an important factor in the development of an ever-widening field of academic theories. The ideas that emanated from the scholars of the *Institute for Social Research*—Critical Theory—continue to influence the Western world today. The borrowing and application of Marx's ideas has become increasingly commonplace—which speaks for the portability and attractiveness of the oppressor/oppressed framework—throughout the world, including in colleges and universities, and it continues unabated.

Where can it be found?

Critical Theory, unfortunately for us, has found its way into myriad organizations. Today it is easily identified everywhere from TV talk shows to 5th grade social studies homework. For many years—decades—critical theorists have been teaching philosophy of education, human development, teacher preparation, and curriculum development courses, among many others. These courses are often mandatory for would-be teachers as they pursue bachelor's and master's degrees in preparation for the K-12 classroom. Pay attention to the use of the words 'power,' 'privilege,' or 'equity' the next time you listen to a speech or read a press release from a large corporation. These are connected to Critical Theory in at least two ways.

First, 'power' and 'privilege' are rhetorical artifacts of Marxian thought based in the insistence on a worldview that categorizes action and individuals as oppressive or oppressed. These ideas have been a permanent fixture in academia since the publication of the *Communist Manifesto* in 1848, but have gained a significant amount of ground in other institutions over the past 5-10 years.

Second, the fluidity of definitions in language is a product of Critical Theory as well as Postmodernism, due to the influence of Friedrich Nietzsche (1844-1900) on both schools of philosophical thought.[81] So, while equity has traditionally meant "interest in," or "fairness," it has come to mean something very different in recent years. It is now used to communicate "equality of outcome"[82] (*for more on this topic, see Chapter 11*).

While there have been radical thinkers for as long as there has been thought, nevertheless, one can find evidence of Critical Theory's influence in modern philosophy wherever edgy ideas are pushed for their own sake:

"For the value of a thought is measured by its distance from the continuity of the familiar. It is objectively devalued as this distance is reduced."[83]

Critical Theory has been preached from the pulpits of Western universities for so long now—nearly 100 years—that its ideas are 'baked into' the American education system. They are so deeply embedded that the very language used to describe concepts, theories, practices, and more are rarely recognized by anyone as having been born of Critical Theory, outside of a post-graduate philosophy of education course.

Among the myriad words in common usage today that have their roots in CT are the universally-valued *equity, trauma-informed, liberatory,* and *diversity.* Most people who use these words are

---

[81] Bronner, S.E. (2017). 26.

[82] GWU. (2020 November 5). Equity vs. equality: What's the difference. Milken Institute School of Public Health. George Washington University. Retrieved on 2021 May 11: https://tinyurl.com/jff8s22x.

[83] Adorno, T.W. (1951). *Minima moralia: Reflections from damaged life.* Verso. Brooklyn. 80.

unable to define them in a way that is consistent with their usage in academic settings. This is worth noting for at least one extremely important reason. The ideologue will attempt to scratch at this by saying that all that *heady academic mumbo jumbo never makes it into the classroom, anyway. So, what's the big deal? Let the Marxist professors have their fun writing articles for journals that no one will ever read.* Here's why all that noise in the echo chamber needs to be taken seriously by the rest of us: It's not an echo chamber they're preaching to—it's America's future educators. It's also America's future curriculum developers. It's also America's future school administrators, state superintendents, and U.S. Department of Education officials. Why does it matter that the meanings of words have been changed by Critical Theorists in Western universities? Because nearly 100 years after *The Frankfurt School* was founded, American K-12 curriculum is riddled with subjective, anti-Enlightenment propaganda.

Who are its advocates and critics?

Chief among the early thinkers of *The Frankfurt School* were Herbert Marcuse and Max Horkheimer.[84] Marcuse (1898-1979) was born in Berlin and, after serving in the German army in World War I, earned his PhD at the University of Freiburg in

---

[84] Ibid.

1922. Six years later, he returned to Freiburg to study under Edmund Husserl[85], completing a habilitation[86] with Martin Heidegger on the ontology of Hegel. Marcuse continued the tradition of his mentors and teachers by further developing the central idea that reality is inaccessible, unknowable. For Marcuse and his colleagues, it wasn't just beauty that was in the eye of the beholder—all of reality was in the eye of the beholder as well. Like many members of the Frankfurt School, Marcuse fled Europe in the years leading up to World War II to escape persecution.

Horkheimer (1895-1973) was a respected, persuasive voice in the fight against reason. He studied under Hans Cornelius at Frankfurt Am Main, graduating with his PhD around 1925[87]. Cornelius trained Horkheimer in the tradition of neo-Kantian[88] thought, which can be fairly accurately summarized with the phrase, *logic and reason are useless tools*. One of Horkheimer's early, and most famous, works, *Traditional and Critical Theory*, provides a kind of philosophical roadmap that the work of the

---

[85] Husserl was a contemporary of Sigmund Freud and they shared a mentor at the University of Vienna, Franz Brentano. Brentano was a major influence on both men's thinking about the nature and reality of the objective world—something that is unknowable; something about which science and empiricism can reveal very little.

[86] A habilitation is similar to a doctoral thesis and is a prerequisite to teaching at the university level in some countries.

[87] SEP. (2013 July 21). *Max Horkheimer.* Stanford Encyclopedia of Philosophy. Retrieved on 2021 May 26: https://plato.stanford.edu/archives/fall2013/entries/horkheimer/.

[88] Möller, P. (n.d.). *Hans Cornelius.* Philolex. Retrieved on 2021 May 26: http://philolex.de/corneliu.htm.

Institute for Social Research would follow for many years thereafter. Most notably, he emphasized the idea that traditional theory doesn't weigh or consider the potential effects of its work on society as a whole. Because traditional theory was responsible for the Enlightenment, and science was a product of the Enlightenment, the whole of modernity was rightly under suspicion. More than that, because the Enlightenment brought individualism and capitalism to life, and these were the cause of so much suffering and blood, the Enlightenment itself is deserving only of disdain and repudiation.[89] So argued Horkheimer.

Proponents of Critical Theory continue to propagate its ideas at universities including Rutgers University's Dr. Stephen E. Bronner who teaches in the Department of Political Science. Bronner teaches courses on *Marxism and Marxist Theory*, *Critical Theory & Society*, *The Politics of Bigotry*, and *Critics of Modernity*, among others.[90] He has won awards from his peers for his contributions to the field of political science and political theory.

Dr. Douglas Kellner has been an employee of University of California-Los Angeles (UCLA) since 1995. Previously, he

[89] SEP. (2013 July 21). *Max Horkheimer.* Stanford Encyclopedia of Philosophy. Retrieved on 2021 May 26: https://plato.stanford.edu/archives/fall2013/entries/horkheimer/.
[90] Rutgers. (n.d.). *Stephen Eric Bronner.* Retrieved on 2021 May 11: https://www.polisci.rutgers.edu/cb-profile/93-ebronner.

taught at University of Texas-Austin where he taught Marxism and Critical Theory from 1973 until 1995. Kellner advocates for a "learning process and relation between student and teacher is rethought."[91]

Dr. Angela Yvonne Davis (b. 1944) is an author, communist revolutionary, radical feminist, professor at University of California at Santa Cruz. Her doctoral advisor was Herbert Marcuse. She carried on the critical theory tradition of 'questioning everything' throughout her career by flouting more than just customs and traditions, but also law and order—she is a radical, after all. She participated in an interview in 2020, during which she briefly reminisced about her time with Marcuse. Calling that experience 'invaluable,' she recalled, "*my philosophical orientation was grounded in critical theory, and... I never seriously considered philosophy except in relation to its potential role in in social transformation.*"[92]

---

[91] Kellner, D. (2003). *Toward a critical theory of education.* Democracy and Nature. 9(1). 51-64. https://doi.org/10.1080/1085566032000074940.

[92] Davis, A.Y. (2020 August 31). *Angela Davis on international solidarity and the future of black radicalism.* Verso. Retrieved on 2021 May 20: https://lithub.com/angela-davis-on-international-solidarity-and-the-future-of-black-radicalism/.

Chapter 4 | The 1960's & Postmodernism

The teacher's purpose is first to show students realize that they live in a pathological system that is marked by power struggles in which the weaker are constantly oppressed, exploited, and taken advantage of by strong groups. One's job as a teacher is next to cultivate the students' identification with those oppressed and exploited groups—which will then make the students into the revolutionaries who will overcome modern society and bring forth a postmodern one.[93]

What is it?

Reality is formed only through language (what we say), and we only ever use language to gain power. The only real thing that truly exists is power and everything anyone does or says (human interactions) can only properly be understood as a struggle for power. Everything is relative, or subjective. There is no objective reality, as postmodernism "den[ies] the universal."[94] This is postmodernism in a nutshell.

---

[93] Hicks, S.R.C., (2019). *The postmodern critique of liberal education*. Reason Papers. 41(1).
[94] Pluckrose, H., Lindsay, J., (2020). *Cynical Theories*. Pitchstone. Durham, North Carolina.

Dr. Catherine McCarthy of University of Iowa explains that it is "...*antithetical to the development of genuine scientific knowledge.*"[95] She continues, "*Postmodernists emphasize culture as the determinative factor in fixing belief*... [and that] *all forms of knowledge, and even scientific knowledge, are mere dogmatically held cultural beliefs*..."

Postmodernism is an attack on the very roots of Western Civilization—reason, science, and individualism. Individualism, the idea that each person is an agent unto themselves; that they can act freely in the world and 'reap what they sow' (for good or bad), is one of the primary insights of the Enlightenment. It also serves as the foundation for Western Civilization today[96]. It undergirds our system of government, our economic, and legal structures. The individual is responsible to make the most of what they have in terms of means and resources. Of course, means and resources vary widely between individuals, even within the same family where siblings—raised in the same home with the same opportunities for education, etc.—end their lives in vastly different positions. For the altruistic and the compassionate, assisting the dispossessed and disaffected is an imperative. Importantly, you don't have to be a compassionate individualist to agree that poor people should be helped.

---

[95] McCarthy, C.L. (2018). History, philosophy, and science teaching. Springer.

[96] Stanford University, (2017). *Enlightenment*, Stanford Encyclopedia of Philosophy, Stanford University. https://plato.stanford.edu/entries/enlightenment/

Proponents of postmodernism seems to be allured by the freedom to question everything. The restrictions of objectivity are replaced by a belief in the relative nature of both truth and reality. Postmodernism is "the Counter-Enlightenment tradition"[97] that has maintained its grip on America's intelligentsia for over 50 years now.

For the believing postmodernist, feelings matter more than 'the truth,' because what's 'the truth,' anyway? If there is no truth, then I get to believe whatever I want and it becomes 'my truth,' which is something that I should speak ('speak your truth'), and something everyone else should care about ('listen to their truth', 'let them speak their truth'). In this way, reality is strictly subjective and relative. As Dr. Christine L. McCarthy rightly notes, *"The body of cultural belief, developed by any sort of method and tested only by its endurance over time, is to be considered, in the postmodern/cultural studies worldview, to be the "science" of that culture."*[98] Postmodernism turns objective reality on its head by claiming that reality exists only within the mind of the individual, and because every individual perceives things differently, there is no knowable reality outside of the human mind.

---

[97] Hicks, S.R.C. (2004). (67).
[98] McCarthy, C.L. (2018). *Cultural studies of science education: An appraisal.* Springer. (99-136).

Even in the absence of a universal, knowable truth, there is still something to strive for; a set of ideals to pursue. You'll recognize these ideals as obvious and universal: diversity, inclusion, equity (DIE). And, we shouldn't be surprised that most parents, school staff and administrators, as well as lawmakers tend to favor programs that carry labels like "diversity" and "inclusion"—at least initially. In fact, you may be one of these stakeholders that supports such programs even at this moment. Programs with names like these are likely motivated most often by a desire to enrich and uplift, or at least I believe that's the case.

Sadly, they rarely accomplish any such thing.[99] We live in a pluralistic society where we're not expected to all think or believe the same things, but we are expected to uphold the rights and freedoms of our fellow citizens. In a monopolistic K-12 school system, there will always be a certain number of families who disagree with the decisions of their local school districts. The Cato Institute maintains a publicly-available online database of conflict over curriculum, policies, and other considerations relative to K-12 education called the *Public Schooling Battle Map*.[100] A quick glance at the map reveals the hundreds of documented cases of conflict in school districts across the

[99] Bregman, P. (2012). *Diversity training doesn't work*. Harvard Business Review, Harvard University. https://hbr.org/2012/03/diversity-training-doesnt-work

[100] Cato Institute. (n.d.). *Public schooling battle map*. Cato Institute. Retrieved on 2021 March 27: https://www.cato.org/education-fight-map

country over these issues, not to mention those that never make the news. These conflicts wouldn't be necessary if parents had education options that met the needs of their students.

Where did it come from?

Postmodernism has a somewhat complicated origin story, as you might expect: *"The key ingredients of postmodernism were laid out by the philosophers of the first half of the twentieth century"*[101] as well as others who prepared the path—among them, Heidegger, Hegel, Kant, Kierkegaard, and Nietzsche. Each of these, in turn, took swipes at the roots of reality. They questioned our ability to know anything through modern science and attacked the very existence of objective fact.

> *"Heidegger attacks logic and reason to make room for emotion, Foucault reduces knowledge to an expression of social power, Derrida deconstructs language and turns it into a vehicle of aesthetic play, and Rorty chronicles the failures of the realist and objectivist tradition in almost-exclusively metaphysical and epistemological terms."*[102]

These individuals laid an axe directly into the roots of the Enlightenment using only words. *"What I say is true because I*

---

[101] Hicks, S.R.C. (2004). (81).
[102] Ibid.

prove that it is—but what proof is there that my proof is true?"[103]

Today, the world benefits from the wisdom of Enlightenment thinkers who developed and used the scientific method to hypothesize, theorize, and then test how those ideas effected objects, processes, and systems in the objective world. That interplay between ideas, actions, and reactions is considered 'objective science' because it is testable and verifiable. Postmodernism offers no comparably robust process of falsifiability. Because it is unfalsifiable, it allows the believer to get away with essentially anything with which law enforcement doesn't take issue. They can choose to believe and advocate for essentially anything because their subjective worldview is just as valid as anyone else's. In fact, one person's 'lived experience' and resulting inclinations in any particular direction are equal in validity to so-called 'empirical knowledge.'

I've often thought the cure for postmodernism might just be two solid years doing manual labor. There's nothing like blood, sweat, and exhaustion at the hands of the natural world that can convince a person that there is a knowable reality. Be that as it may, Jacques Derrida and others asserted that there is no objective truth—again, with the incongruent stipulation that

---

[103] Lyotard, J.F. (1979). *The postmodern condition: A report on knowledge.* In J. Natoli, L. Hutcheon (Eds.), A postmodern reader. (pp. 71-90). SUNY Press.

power is objectively real. Yes, you're right to be confused at the logical inconsistency, but this may help clear that up: postmodernists don't believe that logic is important, or even useful. Of course, this is convenient for them, because they get to make up all the rules as they go along. The Critical Theorists and Postmodernists dismissed logic as an invention of 'mere schoolteachers' and one of their ideological forebears, Friedrich Nietzsche, saw it as a subjective imposition on 'reality.'[104] Vasant Kaiwar, a Visiting Associate Professor of History at Duke University, draws connections between the critical theorists and the postmodernists by noting "…a shift from Marx and Gramsci to Nietzsche and Heidegger, if not Foucault and Derrida."[105] While this is all interesting background on the philosophical origins of postmodernism, the question remains: 'How did this set of ideas that rejects an objective, shared reality altogether come to be taken seriously anywhere outside a philosophy classroom?' A reasonable question, no doubt—pun intended.

Famed scientist/philosopher Thomas Kuhn (1922-1996) and one of his contemporaries, Richard Rorty (1931-2007), had continued the tradition of pushing Kant's *Critique of Pure*

---

[104] Hicks, S.R.C., [@srchicks]. (2021, March 10). *Heidegger explicitly disavows it as an invention of mere schoolteachers. F and D follow Nietzsche in seeing logic as…* [Tweet]. Twitter. https://twitter.com/SRCHicks/status/1369806881162747909

[105] Kaiwar, V. (2015). *The postcolonial Orient: The politics of difference and the project of provincializing Europe (historical materialism).* Haymarket Books. Chicago.

Reason as far as they could. They, along with many others, argued that science is biased from the very beginning of the scientific method. The moment a scientist selects a hypothesis to test, they have loaded the whole process with their values, prejudice, and beliefs—they selected it from all the other possibilities, after all. They could have chosen anything to test, but they didn't, did they? They chose *that*. Kuhn's renown as a scientist gave weight to his philosophical arguments against the availability, or even possibility, of objective facts. Other scientists began to believe this. This adoption of Kuhn's views played at least some role in the adoption of postmodern philosophy in the 'hard sciences.'

All the while, John Dewey, W.E.B. Du Bois, Martin Heidegger, and others were influencing the field of education. Without a doubt, Dewey was most prominent in this regard. Dewey was a pragmatist. He saw the connection between mind and body as equally important constituent parts of the human conception of reality. This allowed him the flexibility to agree with the rationalists and the empiricists at the same time. He didn't have to grant that a scientific experiment that produced the same result 1,000 times consistently was virtually settled, or in any sense 'natural law.' Similarly, he didn't have to accept that our only path to accumulation of knowledge was through reason, though the door was left open for a dash of innate knowledge and inborn intuition. If his position seems like equivocation, that's because it is, in short. Coming by a solid position between rationalism and empiricism isn't something an individual can do over a holiday weekend. Nonetheless, Dewey provided himself with plenty of philosophical cover to make a wide array of claims about how children learn best and how teachers should be trained, etc. Dewey was a highly-sought-after speaker at education gatherings and events. He was widely respected and held responsible positions at several universities including University of Chicago and Columbia. He took a special interest in education, applying his philosophy and psychology background to the teaching of children. In 1897, he published *My Pedagogic Creed*, which outlines his philosophies on education. His ideas and works still have a significant impact on education training and policy in America today. According to Google Scholar, Dewey has been cited over 347,000 times. Dewey had a profound impact on the thinking of Richard Rorty,[106] which, given Rorty's ideas about the nature of reality, says something about how Dewey's philosophy has impacted American educational thought.

Where can it be found?

"...the current teaching standards in the USA call for teachers to embrace a social constructivist view of learning and teaching in which science is described as a way of knowing about natural

---

[106] SEP. (2007 June 16). *Richard Rorty*. Stanford Encyclopedia of Philosophy. Retrieved on 2021 May 25: https://plato.stanford.edu/entries/rorty/.

phenomena and science teaching as facilitation of student learning through science inquiry."[107]

Postmodernism pervades student classrooms from preschool through university.[108] Constructivism, Postmodernism, and Critical Theory (in its various forms and subspecies) are prevalent in learning institutions throughout the West. But this didn't happen by itself, of course. Henry Giroux, a high school social studies teacher who later became a professor of education (Miami University, Ohio; Boston University; McMaster University; Pennsylvania State University), became deeply involved in bringing Critical Pedagogy into U.S. universities—and managed to smuggle in postmodernism, as well. He did this, most notably, in his 1991 book *Postmodern Education: Politics, Culture, and Social Criticism,* which he coauthored with Stanley Aronowitz. He had written about postmodernism in education as early as 1988.[109]

---

[107] Matthews, M. R. (2020). Philosophy and science teacher education. Quoted in The importance of philosophy in teacher education: Mapping the decline and its consequences. Colgan, A.D., Maxwell, B. Routledge. New York. (127).

[108] McCarthy, C.L. (2018).

[109] Giroux, H. (1988). *Border pedagogy in the age of postmodernism.* Journal of Education. 170 (3).

Who are its advocates and critics?

Dr. Henry Armand Giroux of McMaster University is a frequently-cited researcher in the education field. His work has been highly influential among theorists and practitioners from higher education to K-12. His most popular writing among other academics, based on the number of citations (6,649 at the time of this writing), is *Literacy: Reading the word and the world*, a work for which he wrote the introduction, published in 2005. One of his seminal works on postmodernism, *Postmodernism as Border Pedagogy: Redefining the Boundaries of Race and Ethnicity,* is riddled with false claims and hyperbole—but seems to advocate for a goal that is shared by what I believe to be a sizeable majority of people: lifting the dispossessed out of poverty and helping them to secure a sense of dignity and hope. Giroux, along with his longtime friend and mentor Paulo Freire, advocates this be pursued using the rhetoric and tools of Critical Pedagogy (the topic of the following chapter).

One of the major criticisms of the education field is its lack of attention to the philosophy of education—an important component of a discipline's internal culture that could supply the field with guidance, direction, and reasoning skills. These skills, critics argue, would arm educators and those who train them with a defense against anti-intellectual theories that actually do more harm to individuals and society than good. Instead, teacher colleges and university education departments have adopted and borrowed concepts from philosophers and incorporated them in a piecemeal manner. As mentioned above, this has resulted in an often incoherent and disjointed approach to the training of teachers—and, ultimately, the education of children.

Chapter 5 | Critical Pedagogy: Critical Theory in the Classroom

---

"This, then is the great humanistic and historical task of the oppressed: to liberate themselves and their oppressors as well. The oppressors, who oppress, exploit, and rape by virtue of their power, cannot find in this power the strength to liberate either the oppressed or themselves. Only power that springs from the weakness of the oppressed will be sufficiently strong to free both."[110]

What is it?

Students are oppressed and must be freed from their captive state. Teachers can liberate students by teaching them how to "take away the oppressors' power to dominate and suppress," "through transforming action."[111] The critical pedagogue, the teacher who liberates, must first apprise their students of their oppression—a circumstance they are unaware of because of their submersion in an oppressive reality. Teachers who liberate are

---

[110] Freire, P. (1970). *Pedagogy of the oppressed.* Modern Classics. London.
[111] Freire, P. (1970).

radicals, and they must be or they would not be able to free the oppressed students. This is Critical Pedagogy in a nutshell.

To be clear, according to Critical Pedagogy, the oppressors cannot free the oppressed. The energy required to break free from the bondage of the oppressor is only to be found within the oppressed. For the Marxist educator, "…the pedagogy of the oppressed cannot be developed or practiced by the oppressors. It would be a contradiction in terms if the oppressors not only defended but actually implemented a liberating education."[112] The framing of one's reality in terms of oppressor and oppressed is fundamentally Marxist. The word 'Marxist' has become so much of a cliché that it often reflects more poorly on the person using it than the subject. All accusations of hysterical finger-wagging aside, Critical Pedagogy, like Critical Race Theory and their common parent Critical Theory, is literally Marxist in origin, substance, form, and application. When Freire was writing *Pedagogy of the Oppressed* and his subsequent works, almost no one wanted to be associated with communism or communist thought. Today, of course, that has all changed. Radical communists are heralded as virtuous and wise. This certainly holds true in colleges of education, where 'liberative practices' regularly make their way into the curriculum.

Academia is now very well-known for being left-leaning. What is less well-known is that nearly 18% - 25% of humanities and

---

[112] Freire, P. (1970).

sociology professors, respectively, in American universities self-identify as Marxists, according to a 2014 book on the subject.[113] These professors perpetuate the belief that the primary purpose of schooling is emancipation, because a teacher is expected to help "the learner identify real problems involving reified power relationships rooted in institutionalized ideologies which one has internalized in one's psychological history and it is the responsibility of the teacher to provide the conditions in which this can occur."[114]

Importantly, you can't use the tools that created your oppression to create a new system, and you can't use the system you're in. This is why revolutionaries and activists call for a 'dismantling of the system.' All of Western civilization, its institutions, its laws, its values, culture, and norms must be taken apart piece by piece and replaced with the postmodern utopia which will be ushered in with the help of liberated revolutionaries freed from oppression by critical pedagogues.

Critical Pedagogy, like its parent Critical Theory, is internally inconsistent and circular. However, as stated previously, this does not matter since logic and reason don't even function as speed bumps to slow down the claims of these Theorists. For example, Freire claimed that oppressed students need to be

---

[113] Gross, N., Simmons, S. (2014). *Professors and their politics*. JHUP. Baltimore. 33.
[114] Colgan, A., Maxwell, B. (2019). 56.

informed of their oppression, since they aren't able to recognize it on their own (being submersed in it—thus, unaware). For this reason, teachers should wake up their students to their unfortunate reality. An oppressor cannot assist an oppressed student out of their oppression. So, if a teacher is oppressed like their students, they aren't aware of their oppression—rendering them unable to awaken their students. And, if they are oppressors, they are unable to free their students because they lack sufficient energy and power to do so.

Where did it come from?

Pedagogy, or 'the science of teaching,' finds its etymological roots in the Greek 'paidagogos' (παιδαγωγός), meaning 'teacher.' Brazilian philosopher and educator Paulo Freire's (1921-1997) *Pedagogy of the Oppressed*[115] quickly became the lodestar for educators in teacher colleges[116] in the early 1970s.[117] According to a 2016 study, Freire's book is the third-most cited book in all peer-reviewed studies in the social sciences with over 72,000 citations.[118] His name is referenced over 425,000 times

---

[115] https://en.wikipedia.org/wiki/Pedagogy_of_the_Oppressed
[116] Bartlett, L. (2008). *Paulo Freire and peace education*. Encyclopedia of Peace Education. Teachers College, Columbia University.
[117] UNESCO. (2018, November 16) *The relevance of Paulo Freire's work in today's world*. UNESCO UIL, https://uil.unesco.org/adult-education/relevance-paulo-freires-work-todays-world
[118] Green, E. D. (2016) *What are the most-cited publications in the social sciences (according to Google Scholar)?* Impact of Social Sciences

and the term "critical pedagogy" appears another 176,000 times, according to Google Scholar.

Considering the etymology of the word *pedagogy*, 'pedagogy of the oppressed' could be described as: 'the science of the teaching of oppressed peoples.' This is exactly what Freire meant when he titled his 1968 book (translated into English in 1970) of the same name. The obvious next questions become, "who are the oppressed, and who is oppressing them?" For the critical pedagogue, the oppressed are those who are commonly referred to as 'underprivileged.' Defining the 'oppressed' in this way would likely gain a reasonable amount of agreement from a wide range of people. But, the critical pedagogue doesn't stop there. For instance, the Smithsonian Institute, on its website for the *National Museum of African American History and Culture* explains that oppression and 'systems of oppression' may be experienced and felt by anyone in a "non-dominant group." They can be oppressed in various ways, which may come in the "…form of limitations, disadvantages, or disapproval. They may even suffer abuse from individuals, institutions, or cultural practices. "Oppression" refers to a combination of prejudice and institutional power that creates a system that regularly and

---

Blog (12 May 2016). Retrieved on 2021 May 11: http://eprints.lse.ac.uk/66752/.

severely discriminates against some groups and benefits other groups."[119]

Using this definition, the oppressed could include anyone that feels disapproval by someone else specifically because they don't belong to the same group as them. Likely this is where the critical pedagogue begins to lose a significant share of agreement and support for her cause. The truth of the matter is that every individual faces hardship, certainly in the form of disapproval, at several points in their lives. So, this definition is too broad to retain any meaningful amount of agreement. For the believer, however, broad appeal doesn't matter when you have the support of virtually all of the national media outlets as well as the vast majority of the prominent institutions of higher learning. With these two institutions alone, a movement can yell long and loud—which it has and does.

Freire's work spawned a flurry of related and derivative works by other academics, among them, notably, Dr. Henry Giroux. Freire and Giroux became fast friends as they discussed their ideas and worked on projects together periodically. Today, Giroux is recognized as one of the early proponents of Critical Pedagogy. He is also an adherent of Critical Theory and Postmodernism, as mentioned in the previous chapter. His

---

[119] SI. (n.d.). *Talking about race. Social identities and systems of oppression.* Smithsonian Institute. Retrieved on 17 May 2021: https://nmaahc.si.edu/learn/talking-about-race/topics/social-identities-and-systems-oppression.

writings have been cited over 129,000 times according to Google Scholar.

Taken together, Freire and Giroux have had a massive impact on the fields of education and sociology, among others. Whether that impact has been positive is another question altogether. Proponents, of course, will argue that their work has shined a light on the incredible amount of work that needs to be done to relieve suffering and eradicate oppression. Critics will undoubtedly question the premise that oppression can be so widely defined and still retain any amount of usefulness. Regardless of these questions and quarrels, the fact remains that Critical Pedagogy has changed education in America, and it will continue to do so for as long as teachers are trained to view the classroom as the site of liberation from the oppressor rather than as a welcoming and stimulating place of intellectual growth.

Where can it be found?

Paulo Freire's early work, Critical Pedagogy, is required reading in courses for would-be teachers across the country. The ideas contained in the book and subsequent writings on the topic are now found in textbooks, slide presentations, professional development for teachers, and even state and national education policy. State standards for K-12 education are infused with language that was born out of this ideology over the past 50 years. Ideas that elicit the idea of the classroom teacher being simultaneously a student, and vice versa, are scattered throughout curricula, course materials, and learning standards.

"The only advantage in arriving at and maintaining a fixed belief system which is not well-warranted to be true of nature is the fostering of a feeling of solidarity, of community of belief. But false beliefs about the world are likely to lead at some point to actions in the world that fail miserably in achieving the desired goal."[120]

From a strictly practical standpoint, some aspects of his philosophy are difficult to argue with: teachers and students can learn from one another in the classroom, and teachers should use their experiences to inform future practice. Being 'present' for each and every student during the learning process is important and desirable. Again, this isn't just 'okay,' or 'reasonable,' this is *desirable*. It's worth mentioning, however, that these ideas did not originate with Freire. Implicit and explicit references to these concepts are found in religious and philosophical writings dating back millennia.

How about other aspects of his pedagogical model? Often, they're much more difficult to defend. For instance, Freire was a dedicated Marxist and a student of Hegel. Freire's worldview, as a result, framed every interpersonal relationship in terms of

---

[120] McCarthy, C.L. (2018).

power dynamics. Every group or class relationship, from this perspective, must be viewed from within the framework of oppressor and oppressed.

Freire applied this framework to the classroom. Teachers were the oppressors and students the oppressed. In order to deconstruct the oppressive relationship, teachers had to co-create learning with the students, not simply "fill an empty bank."[121] This assertion runs directly counter to the popular model –called "direct instruction"—described and advocated for by E.D. Hirsch, which claims that students must have background contextual knowledge of any particular situation in order to comprehend new material being presented. In other words, a foundation of knowledge needs to be built up, layer upon layer, for a student to understand what they're learning, and that this is best accomplished by a teacher explicitly instructing the student. Additionally, this method assumes that students need to be actively guided and instructed in their learning, rather than relying on their individual preferences. Research has shown this traditional method of instruction to be quite effective.[122]

Who are its advocates and critics?

A variation (sans oppression-framework) of Freire's preferred approach is gaining some momentum among parents and

---

[121] Freire, P. (1970). *Pedagogy of the oppressed.* Modern Classics.
[122] Adams, G.L., Engelmann, S. (1996). *Research on direct instruction: 25 years beyond DISTAR.* Educational Achievement Systems.

educators that removes the formality of a traditional classroom in what is commonly called "student-directed learning."[123] Many Montessori schools and some 'project-based learning" schools use this model as their primary approach—one that undoubtedly works well for many students.

Freire's work is still widely practiced and celebrated.[124] His commitment to uplifting the individual whenever and wherever possible has earned him the respect of allies as well as critics. Well-meaning though his intentions may have been, their various applications have largely led to negative outcomes.

For some, Freire's ideas aren't being implemented quickly or overtly enough for their taste. A 2021 peer-reviewed article in *Race Ethnicity and Education* accuses efforts to advance social emotional learning (SEL) in schools as *"hegemonic miseducation."* The authors advocate, in place of SEL, for the *"pedagogy and psychology of humanization."[125]*

---

[123] Petro, L. (2017). *How to put self-directed learning to work in your classroom.* Edutopia. https://www.edutopia.org/discussion/how-put-self-directed-learning-work-your-classroom

[124] Coles, T. (2014) *Critical pedagogy: schools must equip students to challenge the status quo.* The Guardian. https://www.theguardian.com/teacher-network/teacher-blog/2014/feb/25/critical-pedagogy-schools-students-challenge.

[125] Camangian, P., Cariaga, S. (2021). *Social and emotional learning is hegemonic miseducation: students deserve humanization instead.* Race Ethnicity and Education. DOI: 10.1080/13613324.2020.1798374.

Chapter 6 | Teaching is a Political Act

"... 'cultural literacy' is a hegemonic vision produced for and by the white middle class to help maintain the social and economic status quo. It deliberately fails to consider the values and beliefs of any other particular race, class or gender. Young people who enter the educational system and don't conform to this vision are immediately disadvantaged by virtue of their race, income or chromosomes."[126]

Politicizing Children

"Teaching is a political act" is a euphemism for "we politicize children." A search for the exact phrase "teaching is a political act" on Google returns around 23,900 results. Over the past few years[127] this phrase has surprised and shocked parents as they listened to their children's activist teachers[128] chant, wave

---

[126] Ibid.

[127] Cohen, R. (2018). *Politicized by Trump, teachers threaten to shake up red-state politics.* The Intercept. https://theintercept.com/2018/04/17/teacher-strikes-west-virginia-oklahoma-kentucky-arizona/

[128] Cheng, J., (2019). *Teaching is a political act.* YouTube. https://www.youtube.com/watch?v=LGxBZyAwtjg

posters, write articles[129], and make speeches during strikes and 'walk-outs' (a clever, intentional misnomer that makes strikes legal where, when accurately named, they are not legal). The original quote, from Paulo Freire, reads "Teaching is, after all, a political act."[130] Not only is it political, to believers it *should* be political.[131] Parents are surprised at this phrase because our society doesn't see a school's primary purpose as political indoctrination of students. In fact, history hasn't given us many positive examples of the politicization of children and schools— such examples seem to be isolated to communist dictatorships and the like. Critical pedagogues, ahem, teachers, were trained to enlist children[132] in political activism with an eye toward 'changing the system.' The Black Lives Matter Movement has first-grade teachers leading their young students in songs dedicated to anti-racism.[133] Dozens of articles published in newspapers and education websites give tips and tricks intended to help teachers talk to their students about activism. The popular online marketplace for lesson plans, *Teachers Pay Teachers*, is

---

[129] Waldron, J., (2019). Teachers, don't just shut up and teach. Education Week. https://www.edweek.org/policy-politics/opinion-teachers-dont-just-shut-up-and-teach/2019/07.

[130] Freire, P., (2005). *Teachers as cultural workers: Letters to those who dare to teach.* Westview Press. (Boulder, CO).

[131] Smith, C., (2020, December). *Teaching should be political.* The Atlantic.

[132] Burney, M. (2021 February 4). *Black lives matter movement goes to school to teach students about social justice.* Philadelphia Inquirer. Retrieved on 2021 May 24: https://www.inquirer.com/education/nj-education-black-lives-matter-schools-week-black-history-20210204.html?outputType=amp.

[133] Ibid.

home to over 39,000 products for sale associated with the keyword "activism." A search on the same website for "Martin Luther King" returns a little under 17,000 results, and "Rosa Parks" returns around 6,000. While this is far from a systematic review and comparison, the point remains. Teachers believe that their role is to liberate students through action (e.g. protests, social media,[134] etc.).

The Parkland, Florida shooting at Marjorie Stoneman Douglas High School where former student Nicolas Cruz killed 17 students was undeniably tragic. Too many such incidents occur across the country and around the world. Sadly, we struggle to find actual solutions to violence. Even more disappointing, though, is that victims and those close to them are used as political weapons in the battles between special interest groups. America's education professionals regularly engage in this and they do so unapologetically. It's one of their primary functions, after all. Why shouldn't educators have more say in what they do with your child? A 2013 MSNBC promotional video features Melissa Harris-Perry explaining why parents shouldn't necessarily have complete control over their child's education:

---

[134] Berwick, C. (2021 January 22). *Students excel when they find purpose—so how do we help them?* Edutopia. Retrieved on 2021 May 24: https://www.edutopia.org/article/students-excel-when-they-find-purpose-so-how-do-we-help-them.

"We have never invested as much in public education as we should have because we have this private notion of children. 'Your kid is yours, and totally your responsibility.' We haven't had a very collective notion of 'these are our children.' So, part of it is to break through our kind of private idea that kids belong to their parents, or kids belong to their families, and recognize that kids belong to whole communities...Once it's everybody's responsibility, and not just the household's, then we start making better investments."[135]

Whether the issue is climate change, gun control, or racism, educators have positioned themselves as the experts with the solutions. Mind you, their solutions without fail are aligned wholly with progressivism. You're not supposed to notice that if you disagree with progressive values.

Enlisting Children

There are many organizations even outside of the classroom that are willing to provide tips, curricula, and training on how teachers can encourage activism in schools, as well. The Anti-defamation League (ADL) has built a curriculum specifically for high schools that trains youth to evangelize for the principles of diversity, inclusion, and equity (DIE). They also provide teachers

---

[135] RCP. (2013 April 8). *MSNBC ad: Kids don't belong to their parents, kids belong to communities.* Real Clear Politics. Retrieved on 2021 May 24:
http://www77.realclearpolitics.com/video/2013/04/08/msnbc_ad_kids_dont_belong_to_their_parents_its_collective_responsibility.html.

and administrators with "10 Ways Youth Can Engage in Activism."[136] Such encouragement and training are seen "as an opportunity to "elevate student voice and action as powerful teachable moments."[137] The ACLU provides additional information on their website, with the audience being the students themselves. Speaking directly to students, they answer questions about whether they might be punished more harshly[138] for protesting in favor of one particular issue relative to another. They also host a "Summer Institute" where high school students can spend their off-months in Washington, D.C. honing their "advocacy and activism skills."[139]

Another website outlines a six-step process for becoming a student activist—a heavy lift for a group of individuals who, in most cases, have yet to schedule an appointment with the dentist

---

[136] ADL. (n.d.). *10 ways youth can engage in activism.* Anti-defamation League. Retrieved on 2021 May 24: https://www.adl.org/education/resources/tools-and-strategies/10-ways-youth-can-engage-in-activism

[137] Schulten, K. (2018 March 7). *The power to change the world: A teaching unit on student activism in history and today.* New York Times. Retrieved on 2021 May 24: https://www.nytimes.com/2018/03/07/learning/lesson-plans/the-power-to-change-the-world-a-teaching-unit-on-student-activism-in-history-and-today.html.

[138] ACLU. (n.d.). *Students' rights: Speech, walkouts, and other protests.* American Civil Liberties Union. Retrieved on 2021 May 24: https://www.aclu.org/issues/free-speech/student-speech-and-privacy/students-rights-speech-walkouts-and-other-protests.

[139] ACLU. (n.d.). *High school program.* American Civil Liberties Union. Retrieved on 2021 May 24: https://www.aclu.org/high-school-program?redirect=summer-advocacy-program.

on their own.[140] Not that this should stop anyone from speaking their mind, of course—assuming it actually is their mind that they're speaking.

The School of Education at Loyola University in Maryland is even more public about their support of the teacher's role in activating students on social issues: *"Educators and parents can support students in this worthwhile pursuit [participating in strikes]—changing opinions, and ultimately, bringing about institutional change—by helping them focus their energy and connecting them with levers of power."*[141] This is an invitation to adults to organize children for political purposes and then put them in front of elected and appointed government officials in an effort to advocate for policy changes—most of which have implications about which these kids have little idea. A small fraction of adults understand the mechanics of specific policies at the local, state, and federal levels. To shove children onto a stage where they're to wave their poster or lie down with dozens of their peers in protest is at least irresponsible and at worst

In some schools, teachers don't stop at training students how to be activists and protestors, they actively call for students to

[140] ASO. (2021 April 15). *Student activism in school: Getting your voice heard.* Accredited Schools Online. Retrieved on 2021 May 24: https://www.accreditedschoolsonline.org/resources/student-activism-on-campus/.

[141] Heath, M. K. (n.d.). *Supporting student activism: Tips for teachers and parents.* Loyola University. Retrieved on 2021 May 24: https://www.loyola.edu/school-education/blog/2019/supporting-student-activism.

participate in walkouts.[142]

Priorities, Priorities

Certainly, when math, reading, and writing scores are suffering as they are,[143] the priority should be given to improving on those basics rather than focusing on politics. Perhaps, though, persistent failure is reason enough for an entire profession to move the goalposts from student achievement to "social justice." Parents should be up in arms over the insistence that academic knowledge and skills are being replaced with conversations and exercises that teach kids about 'power' and 'privilege.' The pushback inevitably comes, '*But, seriously, do you think that teachers are cutting into time for math or reading to present lessons on these issues (important as they are)? Of course they're not! After all, teachers can instruct students adequately in all of the basics and still expose children to vital social issues—including the correct positions to take on those issues.*' Ahem. Apparently, they cannot. How often do we hear of the dismal performance of American schools compared with students around the world? How often do we hear of how ill-

---

[142] Moore, A. (2019 December 16). *Black teacher faces backlash after encouraging students to protest racism.* Newsone. https://newsone.com/3896775/black-teacher-faces-backlash-after-encouraging-students-to-protest-racism/amp/.

[143] See website "Nation's Report Card" (https://nces.ed.gov/nationsreportcard/assessments/).

prepared American students are for the 'jobs of tomorrow?' All the time. It's a constant refrain. But, instead of reading replies from leaders in commerce and government that call for an increased emphasis on the basics, we get platitudes extolling the virtues of minors who skip school to wave posters alongside city streets. The price for a willing misplacement of priorities doesn't always demand immediate payment. But, when it does, it most certainly won't forgive the debt—and it won't sleep until it's paid.

In the meantime, universities and national organizations continue to deepen the influence that politics and political activism has in their trainings, seminars, and curricula—all of which end up in your child's classroom. Any amount of surprise at this is only a sign of our ignorance—it's been going on for decades.

In their own words:

Teachers College, Columbia University

"...education is, necessarily, a form of politics. [Freire] averred that schooling is never neutral; instead, it always serves some interests and impedes others. Freire's magnetism lies in his insistence that schooling can be used for liberation, just as it has been used for oppression. He argued that through liberatory education, people come to understand social systems of oppression and equip themselves to act to change those situations. Educators, then, must reconceptualize their labor as political work and

"must ask themselves for whom and on whose behalf they are working."[144]

James Madison University

"...educators shape, develop, and influence student's work, practice, and thinking patterns. The topics and subjects discussed in a class and how they are delivered is a pedagogical choice. Educators need to consider their texts, strategies, policies, and behaviors. Thus, teaching is a political act—highlighting what is not taught as much as what is and identifying aspects of the hidden curriculum in conversation with the overt curriculum."[145]

University of Pennsylvania

"Constructing teaching as the link between public education and the imperatives of democracy, Grande is committed to producing critical educators who understand that teaching is a political act."[146]

National Association of Elementary School Principals

"...teaching is a political act, and to deny beginning teachers the chance to delve into and analyze the political influences that will greatly affect their future careers is, in effect, sentencing them to two-dimensional teacher preparation. This can leave new teachers feeling

[144] Bartlett, L. (2008). *Paulo Freire and peace education*. Encyclopedia of Peace Education. Teachers College, Columbia University.

[145] Streeter, J.R., (2020). Returning to Freire. James Madison University. https://www.jmu.edu/cfi/_files/t-t_20-21/10.08.2020_Returning_to_Freire.pdf

[146] University of Pennsylvania (2020). *Sandy Grande, Professor of Political Science and Native American and Indigenous Studies at the University of Connecticut: "Quechua Geographies: Between Indigeneity and Academia" (LALSES)*. University of Pennsylvania. https://lals.sas.upenn.edu/events/sandy-grande-professor-political-science-and-native-american-and-indigenous-studies

overwhelmed, confused, or in the worst cases, unprepared, unfit, or unwilling to teach."[147]

Henry Giroux, advocating for the continuing politicization of K-12 education in an effort to liberate the oppressed, explained: *"...to the degree that teachers make the construction of their own voices, histories, and ideologies problematic they become more attentive to Otherness as a deeply political and pedagogical issue."[148]* In other words, the more privilege and power teachers recognize in themselves, the more able they are to recognize how students are, and can become, marginalized. This recognition is a necessary precondition to a teacher's efforts to assist in the liberation of underprivileged children. Without it, teachers can only perpetuate oppression—and, no matter how much they may desire it, they'll never have the power necessary to liberate. They can facilitate liberation, but they can't actually liberate—according to Critical Pedagogues.

Again, this approach prioritizes a conversation about power—the fundamental issue for Marxist critiques, in general. That this should even be an issue is a foregone conclusion for the believer. Even self-identifying Marxist parents of students may reasonably

---

[147] Darvin, J. (2012). *Novice teachers need real professional development.* Principal. https://www.naesp.org/resources-principal-marchapril-2012/novice-teachers-need-real-professional-development-2

[148] Giroux, H., (1993). *Postmodernism as border pedagogy.* A postmodern reader. SUNY Press. (New York).

question whether the elementary school classroom is the appropriate place to segregate students and require them to identify as a member of the oppressed or oppressors—or if such a place exists at all.

If internet search terms are any indication of what your PTA-member neighbor is thinking about in their spare time, a historical look at trends of those searches seems to indicate a general increase in interest around words like "whiteness" and "critical race theory."

Figure 1 | *Google search trendline for "Critical Race Theory in Education" (from 2016-2021)*

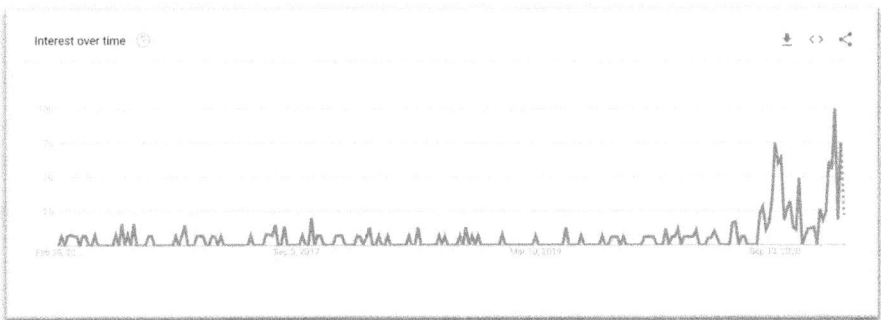

Figure 2 | *Google search trendline for "whiteness" "schools"*

(from 2016-2021)

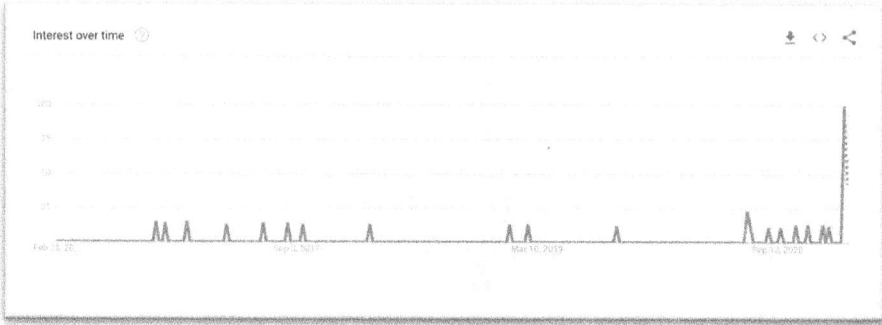

Figure 3 | *Google search trendline for "critical race theory"*

(from 2004-2021)

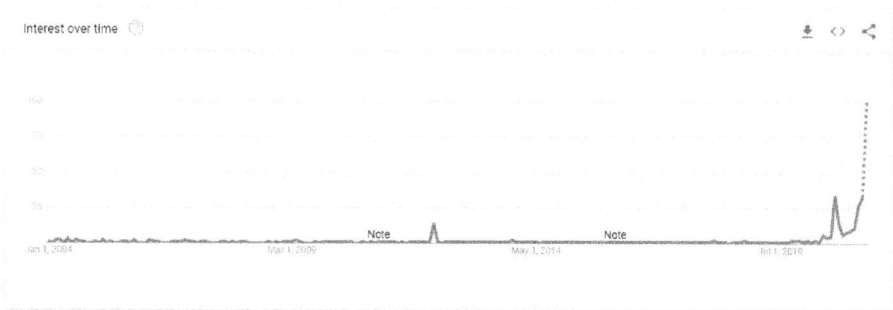

Part 2: And, the Problem?

"Most of what schools teach has no value in the labor market."[149]

Why is all of this such a big deal? Is it really even worth talking or worrying about? Here's why it's a big deal and why you should talk about and worry about it: these theories, which replace a traditional worldview with one that considers everyone and everything through a lens of oppressor vs. oppressed, are proudly illogical. They elevate feelings and perceptions over facts and evidence. No one will deny the importance of emotion—we're human, after all. But, the physical, natural world has become knowable largely to the extent that science has been allowed to pursue facts. As it stands today, society has built up so many artificial, social barriers around specific subjects, that scientists and researchers are effectively disallowed from asking questions that would help us to solve actual problems. Ideologies that gain purchase among the intelligentsia, and are eventually enshrined within law, stand as nearly insurmountable obstacles to inspection and questioning. It's not an exaggeration to point out that reality itself is under attack. Is it possible that all of these

---

[149] Caplan, B. (2018). *The case against education: Why the education system is a waste of time and money.* Princeton University Press. Princeton, New Jersey. (68).

theorists, who benefitted from all of the latest technologies of their time—facilitated by the sciences—could have simply never made the connection between the existence of those amenities and the objective knowledge required to bring them about?

The attack on logic and reason should be motivation enough to at least be skeptical about these ideas. But, there's more. The people that are purported to be aided by the adoption and implementation of CRT and CP, the underserved and minority populations, turn out to be those most harmed. Here's why: telling a child from the time they're young that, due to factors that are so enmeshed into the fabric of reality, they have no hope of getting ahead, is thoroughly demoralizing. It's disempowering. Such an idea takes the abilities, interests, and talents of young children and convinces those kids to drop them, turn around, and toss a lit match over their shoulder on their potential as they walk away. 'Why try? You'll never make anything of yourself, anyway.' It's a travesty and it's been going on for far too long. Now, how much worse is this than telling a child that they perpetuate the suffering of their peers simply by existing? Of course, neither is preferable. Neither should be taught to anyone, let alone children. However, I argue that the damage to kids' psyches is much deeper and long-lasting when adults sell them on the idea that they're oppressed—rather than the oppressor. The child labeled 'oppressor' has personal experience to lean on that serves to invalidate the accusations of demagogic teachers. They can know that they're not actively perpetuating racism or oppression. For the 'oppressed' child, 'the system' is too nebulous to identify which makes refutation very difficult to come by. Anything and everything can be blamed on a vague 'system' when life doesn't go my way. In the 1960s and 1970s, 'the man' was keeping minorities and underserved people down. 'The man' was the oppressor. Today, even the highly-educated cognoscente[150] and politicians perpetuate the idea that 'the system' is keeping the underserved down. And, such claims are difficult to disprove when they're so utterly vague.[151]

The inclusion of Critical Theory and its relatives in classrooms is the equivalent of teaching religion in schools. These ideologies are unfalsifiable. They have mechanisms built into them that completely insulate them from falsification, or even critique. This begs the question: Can we accurately refer to an idea or proposal that is unfalsifiable as a 'theory?' You may believe these things, and you should have every right to believe them and to practice them in your personal life. Brainwashing children, who have no other educational options available to them, into a perpetual state of unearned self-loathing is more than negligent—it's the very definition of evil. If this is the situation

[150] Khalid, A. (2019 October 1). *How white liberals became woke, radically changing their outlook on race.* NPR. Retrieved on 2021 June 16: https://www.npr.org/2019/10/01/763383478/how-white-liberals-became-woke-radically-changing-their-outlook-on-race.

[151] Mansfield, H. (2020 September 18). *The 'systemic racism' dodge.* Wall Street Journal. Retrieved on 2021 June 16: https://www.wsj.com/articles/the-systemic-racism-dodge-11600454532.

you find yourself and your child in, don't expect administrators or teachers to come to your aid. While there are those who would support you in your efforts to protect your child, others will actively fight against you on the pretense that your aversion to their beliefs is evidence of abject bigotry—whether you're black, brown, or white. For example, an online group comprised of nearly 650 individuals in Loudoun County, Virginia coordinated the identification and targeting of a large group of parents in their local school district who opposed controversial racial curriculum and instruction.[152] In Evanston, Illinois, a mother of school-aged children began speaking out against curriculum in her kids' school that she feels is harming students by teaching them that they 'can't get ahead.'[153] If activists insist on teaching kids these ideologies, they will have created the situation that they so passionately decry.

Meanwhile, students can't read or write on grade level. Science scores are no better. We consistently hear that employers complain about the lack of preparation of students. The data seem to indicate they're onto something:

---

[152] Rosiak, L. (2021 March 16). Teachers compile list of parents who question racial curriculum, plot war on them. Daily Wire. Retrieved on 2021 April 17: https://www.dailywire.com/news/loudoun-teachers-target-parents-critical-race-theory-hacking

[153] Fridersdorf, C. (2021 April 3). *The narrative is, 'you can't get ahead.'* The Atlantic. Retrieved on 2021 May 27: https://www.theatlantic.com/ideas/archive/2021/04/black-lives-matter-curriculum-has-unintended-lesson/618501/.

"More than 50 percent of students entering two-year colleges and nearly 20 percent of those entering four-year universities are placed in remedial classes."[154]

Curricula used throughout the West now include truly harmful ideas that are full of factual errors, dogma, logical fallacies, and false dichotomies—like this one: "Helping students see that it is not the Black child who is a criminal, but the larger society that this child has been born into, eludes tidy teaching scripts."[155] The question isn't whether a black child is a criminal due to skin color, nor is it a question of whether the country is inherently evil.

"...the crucial work of educators is to fortify their students, joining them in the quest to make the society into which they were born fully account for the conditions it has created."[156]

This is the problem. Very young students are being taught consistently that they exist within a system that is inherently unjust and that the only way out is to create a new system. The propensity of people with influence and power—often gained

---

[154] Complete College America. (2012 April). Remediation: Higher education's bridge to nowhere. Complete College America. Retrieved on 2021 April 17: https://www.insidehighered.com/sites/default/server_files/files/CCA%20Remediation%20ES%20FINAL.pdf

[155] Smith, C., (December 2020). *Teaching should be political.* The Atlantic. https://www.theatlantic.com/magazine/archive/2020/12/bringing-politics-into-the-classroom/616934/

[156] *Ibid.*

from within the system they claim is unjust and unfair—to encourage outrage and revolution among those less fortunate than themselves, seems all too predictable and almost irresistible. But, it takes a particularly power-hungry individual to sacrifice the truth of their own success, born of hard work and determination, to the idols of power and fame—lying all the while to their followers about the source and price of prosperity. In this way, demagogues perpetuate the misery of those they claim to seek to inspire in the fight for 'liberation.' They turn their attention away from the requirements of skill, competence, and value, and toward a manufactured 'oppressor' from whom retribution is sought. The distance between themselves and their own independence increases. A special power accompanies those who claim victimhood, even where there is none—or no more than anyone else:

"Sometimes the submissive style is actually the most powerful in controlling the course and outcome of a conflict—meekness and humility can be a morally effective strategy and can induce others to work very hard to obtain the submissive disputants' agreement."[157]

Ideologues will use all the tools at their disposal to gain power— the only objectively real thing in life, according to the Critical Theorists, as well as the Postmodernists. Why not feign

---

[157] Meyer, B. (2012). *The dynamics of conflict.* Jossey Bass. San Francisco. 59.

victimhood to prey upon the sympathies of people who can relinquish their power to the oppressed? The particular traits of demagogues have been enumerated by countless people throughout history. An accurate list would certainly include the propensity to 'dehumanize "enemies"', 'resort to indoctrination, not inquiry,' 'seek uniformity and blind obedience,' and 'rely on ideology, not experience.'[158] Many of the harmful ideas that are being propagated today sow division by creating an 'us and them' dynamic in schools. Demagogues who buy into and instruct children in these ways create 'the "other" by indoctrinating the population with a vision that is fragmented and polarized,' additionally, they brand 'anyone who questions the lies on which their propaganda is based as "traitors" or "one of them."'[159]

This is happening in America's classrooms. Students are spending less time on subjects that would increase their competence and knowledge and more time on destructive ideologies. Student achievement is suffering. Crime is increasing. And, the sources of these ideas are only gaining more influence and power. The chapters in this section will explore how these ideas are manifesting and the problems they cause.

---

[158] Gerzon, M. (2006). *Leading through conflict. How successful leaders transform differences into opportunities.* Harvard Business School Press. Boston. (18).
[159] *Ibid.*

Chapter 7 | Student Achievement

"Tis' education forms the common mind,
Just as the twig is bent, the tree's inclined."
- Alexander Pope

When everything is top priority, nothing is.

At best, spending time on neo-racist and woke ideologies in the classroom is a distraction from the core concepts that we expect all children to learn in school. In this best-case scenario, the distraction pulls teachers and students away from reading, writing, arithmetic, and science. These are areas where America's students need more time and help, not less. Wagner and Dintersmith's controversial book *Most Likely to Succeed* asserts, *"Education in the United States is an equal opportunity abuser."* Why would they say such a thing? *"The reality is that obsolete and ill-conceived education priorities impair the prospects of almost all young adults…"*[160] Ill-conceived education priorities is exactly right. Whether the authors were referring to the neo-racist ideologies discussed in this book, I can't say. But, CRT, CT, and their relatives certainly qualify.

---

[160] Wagner, T., Dintersmith, T. (2015) *Most likely to succeed.* Scribner. New York. 53.

The Three R's

For example, the National Assessment of Educational Progress
(NAEP) Long-term Trend Assessment has been administered to
children across American since the early 1970s. The most recent
results for this assessment are from 2012.[161] A quick look at that
measure of student learning shows non-white students making
gains over that 40-year period, narrowing the achievement gap
between themselves and their white peers. At the same time,
employers report having to start from scratch with college grads,
essentially taking the time to help new hires to unlearn what their
minds were filled with in school. This says nothing about the
longstanding trend[162] of grade inflation.[163] Evidence abounds that
student scores are artificially pumped up in order to move kids
along to the next grade, even when they're not ready.[164]

---

[161] NCES. (2012). *NAEP 2012 Long-term trend: Summary of major findings*.
National Center for Education Statistics. U.S. Department of
Education. Retrieved on 2021 May 19:
https://www.nationsreportcard.gov/ltt_2012/.

[162] Trotter, S. (2021 April 24). *Grade inflation is ruining education*. Quillette.
Retrieved on 2021 June 2: https://quillette.com/2021/04/24/grade-
inflation-is-ruining-education/

[163] Wright, B.L. (2019 Feb 13). *Rampant grade inflation is harming
vulnerable students*. National Association for Gifted Children.
Retrieved on 2021 June 2: https://www.nagc.org/blog/rampant-
grade-inflation-harming-vulnerable-high-schoolers.

[164] Papst, C. (2021 June 2). Leaked documents show Baltimore high schoolers
perform math, reading at grade school level. Fox 5 News Baltimore.
Retrieved on 2021 June 3: https://foxbaltimore.com/news/project-
baltimore/city-high-schoolers-performing-math-and-reading-at-
elementary-level?.

In the worst-case scenario, students are trained to see their peers as innately different and unknowable. There is a chasm that is intentionally excavated by curriculum that uses Critical Theory, Postmodernism and their derivatives as its core philosophy. We intuitively know that students who behave poorly don't tend to earn high marks in school. That intuition has been repeatedly confirmed by researchers. It follows logically that if students are openly and actively encouraged by teachers to look down on their classmates based on their melanin levels, they may find it difficult to 'play nice.'[165] If students aren't playing nice because of what the schools are teaching them, their ability to learn is likely to be compromised.

How much time is spent on reading, writing, and arithmetic today vs. 20 years ago? I have searched and searched for the answer to this question and I have yet to find a definitive answer. I'm positive that I am not the first to have thought of the question. It seems like a question that a lot of people would be interested in hearing more about. Why, then, has it not been systematically studied in K-12 classrooms? My guess is that there may be a very particular group of people that absolutely do not want the general public to know how much time is spent on reading, writing, and math.

---

[165] Wentzel, K., Caldwell, K. (1997). *Friendships, Peer Acceptance, and Group Membership: Relations to Academic Achievement in Middle School.* 68(6)1198-1209. https://doi.org/10.1111/j.1467-8624.1997.tb01994.x

(ahem) Teacher unions.

My impression is that we talk about these three core subjects like we really care about them, but once the bell rings and classes start for the day, teachers just don't end up spending as much time on them as they do on other things. And, last I checked, the clock doesn't expand infinitely if you need to fit more lesson content into the same amount of time you've always had.

Student proficiency, as measured by the NAEP, enjoyed steady improvement from the early 1970s until 2012 when reading scores took a turn for the worse.[166] Taken together, American student performance on the NAEP dropped in 2019—the most recent available data.[167]

"Over the past decade, there has been no progress in either mathematics or reading performance, and the lowest performing students are doing worse..."[168]

In other words, in more politically progressive urban areas, where programs informed by and based upon Critical Theory and Critical Pedagogy are much more likely to be implemented, student scores suffer even more.[169] While these ideas are not

---

[166] NCES (2021). *Long-term trends in reading and mathematics achievement.* National Center for Education Statistics. U.S. Department of Education. https://nces.ed.gov/fastfacts/display.asp?id=38

[167] Camera, L., (30 October 2019). *Across the board, scores drop in math and reading for U.S. students.* U.S. News.

[168] Ibid.

[169] https://www.nationsreportcard.gov/

new, they're only now getting widespread attention because more prominent individuals who have a large reach on social media, etc. have begun to speak up and speak against them. Search engine trends for related keywords, as in the case below, were essentially non-existent only ten years ago. Many of these concepts were only known to academics who studied and wrote about them.

Figure 1 | *Google search trendline for "Culturally" "Responsive" "Pedagogy" (from 2004-2021)*

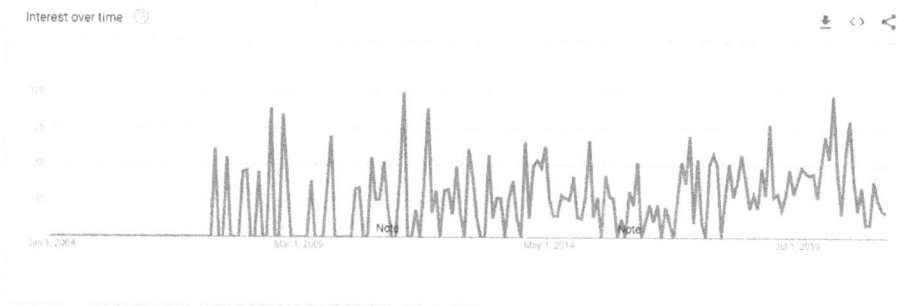

Interest over time

While administrators and teachers should be spending more time on reading, writing, and arithmetic, they're taking more and more away from instructional time to indoctrinate children with controversial ideologies that sow discord and create divisions among classmates. Decades of research has shown that what students need to increase their reading comprehension is additional contextual information—what E.D. Hirsch calls 'cultural literacy.'[170] When we advocate for, or even accept, curriculum that steals time from core subjects in exchange for socially and relationally subversive ideas, we're making a bad bargain. We're polluting the minds and attitudes of children while they're young and unable to reject the nonsense, leading to a deterioration in their disposition to the acquisition of knowledge, not to mention interpersonal relationships:

> *"School success does not seem to depend on the physical condition of the home or of the school; it is more profoundly related to attitudes toward the dominant culture on the part of the parents, the students, and the teachers. Attitudes are critical."*[171]

Let's dream for a moment about what school would look like if we could peel back all of the ideology and dogma that has been building and growing in America's schools for over 100 years now. Let's pretend that students went to school to learn facts and the truth—yes, the whole truth, warts and all. That truth, those facts, and those warts aren't presented to the students as reasons they can't or won't succeed in life. They're also not used as bludgeons on kids who are labeled 'oppressors.' This is our hypothetical fantasy education setting for kids from the age of 5 to 18.

---

[170] Hirsch, E.D., (1987). *Cultural literacy: What every American needs to know*. Vintage. New York. (3).
[171] Patterson, O., (1980). *Language, ethnicity, and change*. Journal of Basic Writing. 3(1) 62-73.

Now, three questions about the details of this hypothetical:

- How proficient are teachers at core subjects?
- What involvement will parents have in the education of their children?
- Do these matter?

Teacher Proficiency

Achievement in math, specifically, seems to be closely related to the subject area abilities of the teacher.[172] That begs the question then, how many teachers are actually good at math, in real life—or at least good enough to help students learn what they need to learn to be proficient? There are two ways we can look at this: the teacher's proficiency, and their students' performance in math. Exams are supposed to tell us the answer to the second question. But, we have comparatively little information available about teacher proficiency. Let's explore this question about teacher proficiency first.

> *An overview of those studies of teachers' mathematical knowledge—elementary and secondary, preservice and experienced—reveals pervasive weaknesses in U.S. teachers' understanding of fundamental mathematical ideas and relationships.[173]*

---

[172] Hill, H. C., Rowan, B., & Ball, D. L. (2005). Effects of Teachers' Mathematical Knowledge for Teaching on Student Achievement. *American Educational Research Journal, 42*(2), 371–406. https://doi.org/10.3102/00028312042002371.

[173] Ding, M. (2007). Knowing mathematics for teaching: A case study of teacher responses to students' errors and difficulties in teaching equivalent fractions. Dissertation. Texas A&M.

There is an apparent mismatch between the capabilities of the average teacher and the education needs of the students. People much smarter than me have suggested myriad solutions to this problem, many of which are worth investigating further. One popular approach is described in E.D. Hirsch's *The Schools We Need*, which incorporates a traditional school-wide curriculum and robust parent communication plan wherein teachers provide regular and frequent updates on student progress.[174] There are thousands of such schools now throughout the United States, with various levels of success at implementation of the model.

Another teaching method that has gained traction in recent years is project-based learning, or PBL. This takes Dewey's pragmatism to its logical end by giving students additional discretion regarding what they learn and encouraging hands-on work to facilitate 'deep learning.' Students in PBL schools will often work in small groups on projects that focus on a theme that is shared between study subjects. For instance, the core-subject teachers for eighth-grade students will together coordinate a theme for their students whose projects will be informed by math, science, and history. The English teacher will assign students work that is intended to be used for their projects.

Regardless of the instructional method that any given school pursues, there will be some students who are well-suited to it,

---

[174] Hirsch, E.D. (1996). *The schools we need and why we don't have them.* Anchor. New York. (62).

and others who are not. For those children who are a match for the method, the fact remains that math teachers need to know math, English teachers need to know English, and so on. A great curriculum with a wonderful parent communication regimen will not make up for subpar teaching. On the other hand, stellar teaching can not adequately fill the gap created by subpar curriculum. There are certain components of a great education that are vital to learning. One additional variable that seems to make a difference in the learning of children is teachers' expectations of them. We know instinctively that when people hold us to a particular standard, we are often motivated to live up to it. It looks as though this applies to students learning science.[175] Why should we think any other subject would be any different? The problem is, we do, and when we do, children suffer. This is what has been called 'the soft bigotry of low expectations.'

Competent and caring educators have the ability to change students' lives. Appropriately-oriented and competently-staffed schools are the keys to a successful K-12 education system. A crucial element of appropriate orientation is shedding directives that do nothing to improve the learning or life outcomes of students. The first things to go should be extraneous curricula, but nothing should be ahead of destructive, disempowering

---

[175] Angle, J., Moseley, C. (2010). *Science Teacher Efficacy and Outcome Expectancy as Predictors of Students' End-of-Instruction (EOI) Biology I Test Scores.* School Science and Mathematics. 109(8) 473-483.

worksheets, lesson plans, and activities. Teachers and administrators would do well to take the Hippocratic oath and commit to 'first, do no harm.'

Parent Involvement in Education

I have yet to meet a person who honestly believes that parent/family involvement in the education of children does either (a) no good, or (b) harm. There's good reason for this consensus: they're right. Parent involvement in their children's education makes a difference. A notable study completed in Chicago in the late 1990's showed that students who received support, encouragement, reminders, and attention from their parents to complete schoolwork, read, study, etc. improved their test scores significantly. By every measure, the study was a success.

> *"...the time, effort, and commitment required from all stakeholders to build a strong parental involvement program is indeed offset by the improvement in students' academic performance and attitude toward learning."*

The authors lamented, however, *"...the only serious mistake we made was not implementing a structured parent involvement program years ago."*[176]

---

[176] Hara, S.R., Burke, D.J. (1998). *Parent involvement: The key to improved student achievement.* School Community Journal. *8*(2), 9-19.

The growing awareness of hot-button issues in education among the general public is important, if only from a parent involvement standpoint. Teachers and administrators have periodically complained about how little interest and attention parents give to the education of their children. They may not like the reason for the sudden involvement, but there is obviously a lot of interest and concern across the country right now.[177] Concerns centering on the appropriateness of the curriculum used in schools aren't likely to lighten up anytime soon. As frustration with the intractability of teacher-union-supported school boards mounts, parents will increasingly advocate for additional education options for their kids. School choice measures are only likely to grow in popularity among voting constituencies. While the motivation for that freedom couldn't have been predicted by anyone ten years ago, the students stand to benefit regardless of the cause of the expansion of options. Parental involvement on a mass scale started in 2020 with widespread school closures and debates over mask mandates. It will continue into the foreseeable future because parents just don't trust that teachers and administrators aren't undoing at school what the parents are trying to accomplish at home. They don't believe that their family's values are being upheld and

---

[177] Adams, L. (2021 June 2). *Douglas County School District's equity policy keeps drawing parent blowback.* Colorado Sun. Retrieved on 2021 June 2: https://coloradosun.com/2021/06/02/douglas-county-schools-equity-policy/.

supported in the classroom. With the ubiquity of CRT, it's easy to see why families are skeptical.

Chapter 8 | Crime, Teen Pregnancy, and Unemployment

"...not all school systems equally contribute to the public good. Indeed, the evidence shows school choice does more to cut crime than residentially-assigned public schools."[178]

Crime

The data on reading comprehension, math skills, and life outcomes is overwhelmingly one-sided, and anyone who pays any amount of attention to these data knows it. Further, a study performed in 2004 concludes, "low literacy is associated with several adverse health outcomes."[179] But, literacy and numeracy do far more than positively impact personal health.

In 2019, according to the U.S. Office of Juvenile Justice and Delinquency Prevention, 696,620 teens were arrested for crimes

---

[178] DeAngelis, C. (2019, July 2) Yet another study shows school choice programs reduce crime. Cato Institute. Retrieved on April 8, 2021: https://www.cato.org/commentary/yet-another-study-shows-school-choice-programs-reduce-crime

[179] DeWall, D.A., et al. (2004) *Literacy and health outcomes: A systematic review of the literature*. Journal of General Internal Medicine. 19(12): 1228–1239. doi: 10.1111/j.1525-1497.2004.40153.x

ranging from murder to gambling.[180] While teen crime rates have generally been on the decline over the past 25 years, there are some troubling trends in specific areas: "Arrests for aggravated assault doubled among preteens between 1980 and 2006, while rape arrests increased by 60 percent."[181]

"The squalor of England is not economic but spiritual, moral, and cultural."[182]

Unfortunately, it seems the same could be said about the United States, where there's more to the perpetuation of poverty and disadvantage than individual bank account balances. Our insistence on taking more and more time away from education in core subjects that prepare children with foundational knowledge that ultimately leads to productive and gainful employment is criminal. Especially so when we replace those subjects with pernicious ideologies that characterize people as allies or enemies based primarily on their melanin levels. So, we remove the content that will help them, if not altogether, certainly portions of it, and fill that time with content that will most certainly harm them. If the price to be paid for this negligence

[180] OJJDP. (n.d.). Estimated number of juvenile arrests. Statistical Briefing Book. Retrieved on April 8, 2021: https://www.ojjdp.gov/ojstatbb/crime/qa05101.asp

[181] Butts, J., Snyder, H. (2008). Arresting children: examining recent trends in preteen crime. Chapin Hall Center for Children, University of Chicago.

[182] Dalrymple, T. (2003). *Life at the bottom: The worldview that makes the underclass.* Ivan R. Dee. Chicago.

were imposed immediately, ideologues might be held to account. We won't know what the demagogues posing as teachers will have actually done to children for some years, including how communities and our society as a whole will be affected. It seems unlikely, though, that crime will be reduced when crimes should certainly be redefined to include a component that accounts for the ethnicity of the so-called 'victim.' Certainly, the perpetrator shouldn't be punished for mugging an oppressor. Such an act would only be just, after all. Similarly, who is anyone to say that 'unemployment' is a bad thing, when the unemployed are so often also counted among the 'oppressed.' Any overlap between the two categories should be taken into consideration and a new term should be added to remove the stigma from those who are only receiving their due from their 'oppressors.' Such support couldn't be called 'employment,' and definitely not 'welfare recipients.' They're claiming what is rightfully theirs from their oppressors, and finding liberation in the process. This is the view of the believer. Having said all this, it goes without saying that people who lack the resources needed to live a good, healthy, honest, decent, and happy life need those resources. We can help them to get those resources using interpersonal, economic, and political means. The question isn't really a matter of who needs assistance, but what kind, and from what source. This is where conversations often stall out. So, we take these bit by bit and issue by issue. One of these that is getting more traction in recent years, and certainly expedited by the global COVID-19 pandemic, is educational freedom. School choice.

Every[183] study[184] that has been performed to determine the effects of school choice on crime has come up with the same result: giving families a choice of education provider reduces criminal behavior.

Teen Pregnancy

The challenges that a young mother will face in life, regardless of her situation, are immense. A great deal of research and attention have been focused on those challenges with the hope that resulting policy prescriptions can help to further reduce unneeded suffering and trauma, as well as the number of unwanted children. Fortunately, teen pregnancy rates have been trending generally downward since 1960.[185] Yes, the overall trend is good. Having said that, the numbers warrant a closer look.

---

[183] DeAngelis, C. (2019, July 2).

[184] McEachin, et al. (2020). *Social returns to private choice? Effects of charter schools on behavioral outcomes, arrests, and civic participation.* Brown University. EdWorking Paper 19-90.

[185] Child Trends. *(2019). Teen births.* Retrieved on 2021 June 2: https://www.childtrends.org/indicators/teen-births.

"In 2017, a total of 194,377 babies were born
to women aged 15–19 years…"[186]

What this data does not include is births to women under the age of 15 and the total number of abortions and miscarriages—both of which must be included in 'total teenage pregnancies.' About 324,000 women under the age of 20 were pregnant in 2017. About 80,000 of those ended in abortion and slightly over 47,000 of them were miscarried.[187] While the difficulty and complexity of assisting teenage mothers is a huge problem in itself, teen pregnancy is, by definition, generational. There are the children of those teen mothers to consider, as well. The National Center for Health Statistics has found that children who are born to teenage mothers are at a much higher risk of committing crime, having health problems, being unemployed as an adult, doing jail or prison time, and giving birth as a teenager themselves.[188]

We hear about the cycles of suffering and poverty that are created through various personal actions—often substantially facilitated[189] and/or assisted by government policies.[190]

---

[186] CDC. (2019 March 1). *About teen pregnancy.* Centers for Disease Control. Retrieved on 2021 June 2: https://www.cdc.gov/teenpregnancy/about/index.htm.

[187] GI (n.d.). *Data center: Teen pregnancies.* Guttmacher Institute. Retrieved on 2021 June 3: https://data.guttmacher.org/states/table.

[188] Martin, J. A., Hamilton, B. E., & Osterman, M. (2018). *Births in the United States, 2017.* NCHS data brief, (318), 1–8.

[189] Burke, L., Butcher, J. (2020). *The Not So Great Society.* Heritage. Washington, D.C.

[190] Teitler, J. O., et al. (2009). *Effects of Welfare Participation on Marriage.* Journal of Marriage and the Family, *71*(4), 878–891. https://doi.org/10.1111/j.1741-3737.2009.00641.x.

These individuals are sincerely struggling through everyday realities from which they need relief. Providing that support is something that needs to happen, without question. Equally crucial is the urgent need to stop the cycle that too often results in children repeating the mistakes of their parents. Sadly, we have yet to come up with and administer the panacea that would allow for a fresh start for children in these situations.

> *"Children of teen mothers perform worse on many measures of school readiness, are 50 percent more likely to repeat a grade, and are more likely than children born to older mothers to drop out of high school."*[191]

The longer a female student stays in school, the less likely[192] she is to become pregnant: education seems to have an ameliorating effect on teen pregnancy.[193] Moreover, if students are fortunate enough to attend a high-performing charter school, teen pregnancy rates are decreased by over ten percentage points.[194] 'Stay in school, kids' is just as important today as it was in the

---

[191] NCSL. (2013 June 17). *Postcard: teen pregnancy affects graduation rates.* National Conference of State Legislatures. Retrieved on 2021 June 3: https://www.ncsl.org/research/health/teen-pregnancy-affects-graduation-rates-postcard.aspx#:~:text=Only%2040%20percent%20of%20teen,finish%20college%20by%20age%2030.&text=Children%20of%20teen%2 0mothers%20perform,drop%20out%20of%20high%20school.

[192] Dobbie, W., Fryer, R. G., (2015). The medium-term impacts of high-achieving charter schools. Journal of Political Economy. 123 (5)

[193] Alzúa, M.L., Velázquez, C., ⬚2017⬚. *The effect of education on teenage fertility: causal evidence for Argentina. IZA J Develop Migration* **7**, 7. https://doi.org/10.1186/s40176-017-0100-8

[194] Dobbie, W., Fryer, R. G., (2015).

public service announcements during 1980's Saturday morning cartoons. The more encouragement and support we can give to students during their K-12 experience, the better they fare in adulthood. Proper encouragement and support for children necessarily precludes disempowering and demeaning ideologies.

Unemployment

Unemployment rates among college graduates are always significantly lower than all other groups. The highest unemployment rates, by education level, are seen among people with less than a high school diploma.[195]

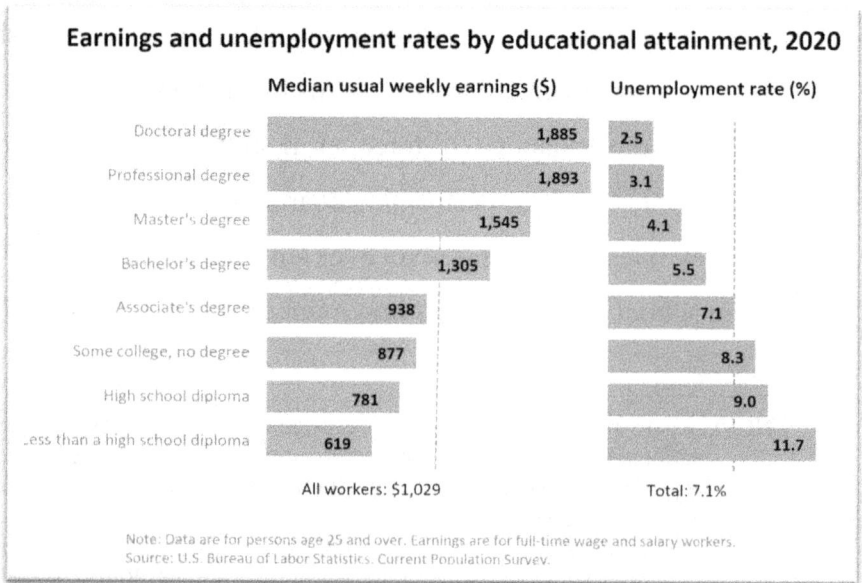

Earnings and unemployment rates by educational attainment, 2020

	Median usual weekly earnings ($)	Unemployment rate (%)
Doctoral degree	1,885	2.5
Professional degree	1,893	3.1
Master's degree	1,545	4.1
Bachelor's degree	1,305	5.5
Associate's degree	938	7.1
Some college, no degree	877	8.3
High school diploma	781	9.0
Less than a high school diploma	619	11.7

All workers: $1,029   Total: 7.1%

Note: Data are for persons age 25 and over. Earnings are for full-time wage and salary workers.
Source: U.S. Bureau of Labor Statistics. Current Population Survey.

[195] BLS. (2021). *Education pays: Earnings and unemployment rates by educational attainment, 2020.* Bureau of Labor Statistics. Retrieved on 2021 June 3: https://www.bls.gov/emp/chart-unemployment-earnings-education.htm.

One of the true joys in life is learning new and useful things. That can mean anything from economics and science to woodworking and welding. We have a severe problem in America that we have made a particular point to worsen. A significant proportion of all jobs open in today's labor market do not require a bachelor's degree and, at the time of this writing, there are over 8.1 million openings in the U.S. to fill.[196] To be clear, this does not mean that they don't require intelligence or initiative. Further, many of these jobs pay a lot of money—more than the median U.S. household income. For decades, we've downplayed and degraded the trades. We've lied to kids about the value of jobs in these fields. On this front, we can and must do better. Society needs the service sector to function properly. Proper function requires skilled individuals in the trades. This is one huge opportunity for today's youth to grab hold of and pursue. It's part of the formula, but not all.

For the 13 months ending in April 2021, the youth (ages 16-19) unemployment rate averaged 22.2%. About one out of every five teens that were actively looking for a job, weren't able to find one. Employed teens also commit far fewer crimes—even if they're only employed during the summer. The positive effects on behavior seem to last far beyond the time they're working.

---

[196] BLS. (2021 May 11). *Job openings and labor turnover summary.* Bureau of Labor Statistics. Retrieved on: 2021 June 3: https://www.bls.gov/news.release/jolts.nr0.htm.

"...a relatively short (and inexpensive) intervention like an eight-week summer jobs program can have a lasting effect on teenage behavior. And it lends empirical support to a popular refrain by advocates: "Nothing stops a bullet like a job."[197]

Summer jobs for youth seem to have the same effect in Boston as they do in Chicago, where crime rates dropped by an average of 44%. There's another benefit that is worth paying attention to: employment brought about crime reductions that "...*were particularly pronounced among African- American and Latino males.*"[198] Why is this important? Because, "...*young people of color are more likely than their white peers to be arrested for violent crimes.*"[199]

The connection

All of this is interesting in a sad and disappointing way, but what does it have to do with harmful ideologies in schools? Fair question. Critical Race Theory and Critical Pedagogy, in particular, teach that underprivileged populations are oppressed

---

[197] Badger, E. (2014 Dec 8). *Chicago gave hundreds of high-risk kids a summer job. Violent crime arrests plummeted.* Washington Post. Retrieved on 2021 June 3: https://www.washingtonpost.com/news/wonk/wp/2014/12/08/one-cheap-way-to-curb-crime-give-teens-a-summer-job.

[198] Modestino, A.S. (2017 December). *How can summer jobs reduce crime among youth: An evaluation of the Boston summer youth employment program.* Brookings Institute.

[199] *Ibid.*

by 'the system.' The system is government, capitalist economies, corporations, even social norms. In schools, CRT and CP dictate that if teachers aren't liberating, they're oppressing. If the demagogues are successful in getting people to believe them (and they are), examples of individuals improving their condition will become increasingly rare. Why, if you believe all of human construction is set against you—including roads and highways[200]—would you expend any extra effort to change something so far beyond your individual strength and capacity? These ideologies disempower further the already underserved. Critical Race Theory, Critical Pedagogy, Critical Theory, and Postmodernism perpetuate and exacerbate tragedy. They are the latest in a long line of Potemkin Villages constructed by education theorists who don't mind experimenting on other people's children. The promises of a utopia are, in reality, hollow facades—but worse still because they don't just disappoint. They increase the suffering of the believer.

Don't be surprised to find correlations between the prevalence of CRT-based curricula in schools and increasing rates of crime, teen pregnancy, and unemployment. There is every reason to believe they are connected.

---

[200] Malanga, S. (2021 April 19). *The agenda behind Buttigieg's claim that 'highways are racist.'* Wall Street Journal. Retrieved on 2021 June 3: https://www.wsj.com/articles/the-agenda-behind-buttigiegs-claim-that-highways-are-racist-11618847867.

Table 1 | *Unemployment rates by education level*[201]

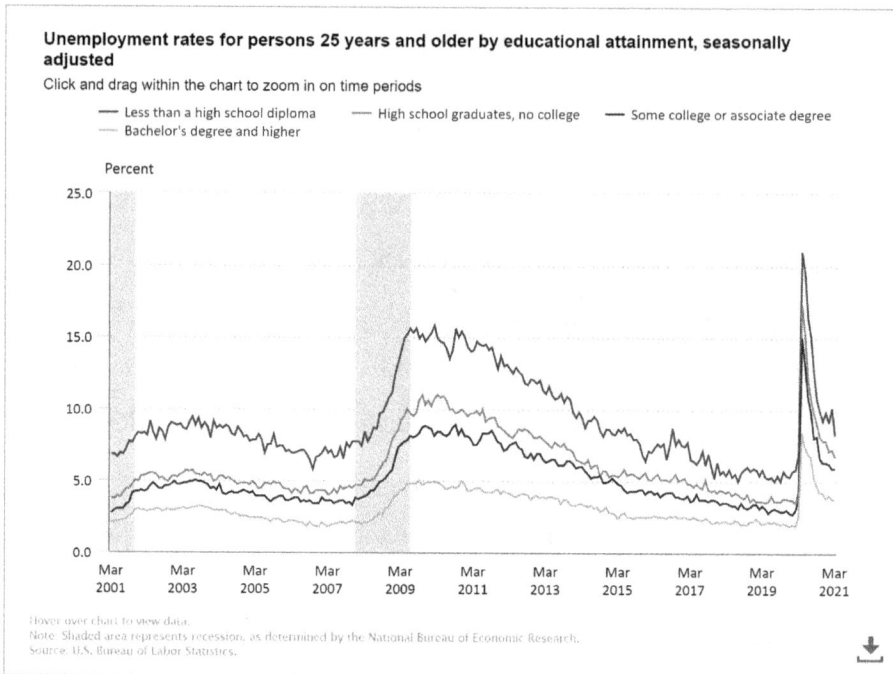

Unemployment rates for persons 25 years and older by educational attainment, seasonally adjusted

Click and drag within the chart to zoom in on time periods

— Less than a high school diploma   — High school graduates, no college   — Some college or associate degree
— Bachelor's degree and higher

Percent

Hover over chart to view data.
Note: Shaded area represents recession, as determined by the National Bureau of Economic Research.
Source: U.S. Bureau of Labor Statistics.

---

[201] Statista. (2021). *Unemployment rate in the United States from 1992-2020, by level of education.* Statista. Retrieved on 2021 June 3: https://www.statista.com/statistics/232942/unemployment-rate-by-level-of-education-in-the-us/.

Table 2 | *Unemployment rates by race*[202]

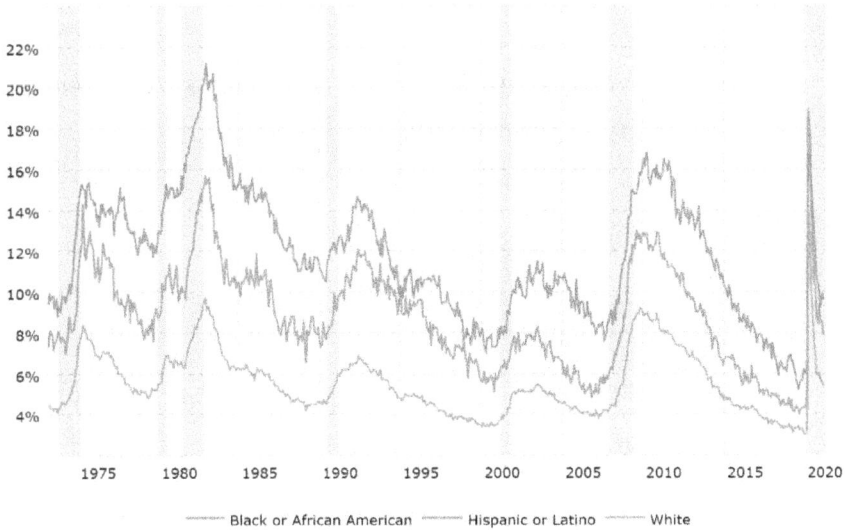

(Legend: Black or African American — Hispanic or Latino — White)

---

[202] Macrotrends. (2021). *Unemployment rates by race.* Macrotrends. Retrieved on 2021 June 3: https://www.macrotrends.net/2508/unemployment-rate-by-race.

Chapter 9 | Ideologies Aren't Solutions

*"Since the sixties whites have had to prove a negative—
that they are not racist—in order to establish their
human decency where race is concerned."*[203]

Intent over impact

Proving the negative—that one isn't racist—hasn't seemed to
work out extremely well for progressive whites, in particular.[204]
Instead of continually trying to perform that impossible feat,
they've found another new, novel way of gaining moral
authority: openly admit your racism, then accuse anyone who
doesn't do the same, of racism (admitted racism is much more
acceptable than denied racism, according to them). The position
of these ideologues is that all white people are racist. How can it
be otherwise when they've grown up in a systemically racist
country where they continuously benefit from their whiteness?
Honest and aware whites admit their racism. Ignorant or evil
whites deny it. Consider, for just a moment, what this kind of

---

[203] Steele, S. (1999). *A dream deferred. The second betrayal of black freedom
in America.* Harper Perennial. New York.

[204] Dupree, C.H. (2018, November 15). *White liberals present themselves as
less competent in interactions with African-Americans.* Yale Insights.
Retrieved on April 7, 2021:
https://insights.som.yale.edu/insights/white-liberals-present-
themselves-as-less-competent-in-interactions-with-african-
americans.

thinking does to children and adolescents who, at their age, are less sure of themselves and still trying to find their footing in life. Consider what it does to otherwise normal and healthy relationships between people with varying levels of melanin in their skin. The people who believe in and advocate for these cynical theories[205] seem to have every confidence that if only all children could be taught 'their truth,' social justice could be won. Equity would reign. Joy would abound. Utopia would be achieved.

For the ideologue, intent matters more than impact.

Here is the problem, however. Advocates make assertions and predictions, but provide no evidence that might win additional support for their cause. We're expected to simply take their word for it. Implementing materials and programs based on CRT, CT, and related philosophies on a wide scale, which is currently happening, is not just ill-advised—though it certainly is that. There is no reason for anyone to believe that such interventions will produce the desired results. Assuming the desired result of these ideologies is to foster diversity, systematize inclusion, and achieve equity at a societal level, among other goals, why should anyone simply take someone's word that Critical Theory can get us there? Even if we accept and espouse the goals as the

---

[205] Pluckrose, H., Lindsey, J. (2020). *Cynical theories*. Pitchstone. Durham, NC.

ideologues define them, attempts at social engineering go wrong—not right—as a rule.[206]

Because proponents have no way to convince us, specifically that part of us that relies on and yearns for rationality and logic, of their ideas, they moralize them. They purposely misuse and redefine words. If everyone already agrees that 'inclusion' is a good thing (no one likes to be excluded, and excluding others unjustly is morally wrong), then just change the meaning of the word so that anyone who disagrees with the worksheet, the discussion, or the curriculum that is implemented to increase that desirable characteristic/outcome looks immoral. This absolves the advocate of the burdens and delays of research and studies on the outcomes of such implementation while making resistance to their prescriptions socially unacceptable. In this way, the ideologue can say and do whatever they like and enlist the support of large proportions of society for their ideas. These supporters will play another important role among their peers on behalf of the ideologues: enforcement. Shelby Steele's books *Shame* and *White Guilt* look at this phenomenon from the race relations perspective in depth. We have every reason to continue to pursue equality and justice, as well as to ensure that we don't repeat the horrific errors of the past with regard to minorities. The vast majority of Westerners agree on this point, which

---

[206] See McCord, J., McCord, W. (1959). *A follow-up report on the Cambridge-Somerville youth study.* The Annals of the American Academy of Political and Social Science. 322(89-96).

accounts for the ongoing and consistent efforts to enact laws, policies, etc. that foster absolute equality. It also accounts for the current success of ideologies that abuse that shared desire in the (softly whispered) name of ending 'geocidal capitalism,' 'individualism,' and 'traditional civil rights.'

It's not you, it's the system

Along with its corollary, 'you're perpetuating a harmful system,' 'it's not your fault, you're just being victimized by a system that was designed to oppress you' are two sides of a false dichotomy—based on a false premise—that has slowly gained a stranglehold on Western society. They are verbal representations of an intentional separation of all people into groups of oppressors or groups of oppressed. Today's popular ideologies remove all personal responsibility from 'oppressed groups.' However, in its currently popular form, this reprieve can only be granted to the degree that an individual is oppressed. Victimhood is measured along three primary identity characteristics: race, gender, and sexual orientation. It has become nearly taboo to ascribe any inadequacy—any whatsoever—to someone who qualifies for a higher degree of victimhood than you yourself do. In this way, the West has pathologized social feedback. You can't tell me when I'm wrong, unless my intersectional identity (white, cisgender, heterosexual males are most privileged) exposes me to criticism and reprimand.

In late 2021, I spoke with Christine Sefein, a former professor of clinical psychology at Antioch College. I wondered what critical social justice ideologies are doing to children's minds. During our conversation, she explained the science behind brain development and what the introduction of these ideas to young children might cause. I've been studying CRT and its relatives for several years now and these ideas have much more potential for long-term, extreme damage than even I understood. Of the many deeply disconcerting effects she explained, two were particularly egregious. First, many people know that the human brain isn't fully developed until about the age of 25. More specifically, the brain's neural pathways are being built at a high rate from infancy, through adolescence, and they slow as you reach your mid-20s. Of course, we continue to create those connections, but at a much slower rate, throughout our lives. We can 'unlearn' things, but we all know how difficult that can be, especially as we grow older. Here's the problem: the average school-aged child spends more weekday hours at school than they do at home. Even when they're not 'receiving instruction,' they're learning—they're building their neural pathways.

What if you send your child to a school where the administrators, teachers, and staff, all believe that the most important things your child needs to know are that they're never going to truly succeed in life because racism is 'permanent and ubiquitous?' When they come home to you each afternoon, you have to tear up the pathways their teachers created and build new ones—every day. And, you have less time to do it because they spend more hours at school than home in a normal school week. If you miss some, or if your child believes their teacher knows more than you do, those neural pathways will stick. Christine also shared that because our need for peer acceptance begins around the age of 10, even the kids that don't necessarily buy into their teachers' ideologies are likely to 'go along to get along.'

We use our neural pathways as a foundation for action. If I've been told often enough that I'll never become a lawyer, like Ndona Muboyayi's son, and I build up that belief in my mind, why should I even try? This is the psychological explanation for why CRT is disempowering for anyone that's not 'white-presenting.' Of course, the same applies for white children, but in reverse. White kids are told that they are the oppressors, just by virtue of their skin color. They may not ever say or do anything that's directly harmful to 'black and brown' people; they don't have to in order to perpetuate white supremacy. Simply being white is enough. Imagine what neural pathways they're building at a school that teaches lessons that encourage so-called 'diversity, inclusion, and equity,' or 'social-emotional learning.' So much of what they teach schoolchildren presupposes systemic racism and everyone's participation in it—either as oppressed or oppressor.

Christine shared with me that she knows individuals who, as practicing counselors and therapists, refuse to provide services to people based solely on their politics—and not because they simply disagree strongly. They won't serve them because they 'feel unsafe.' Think about this for a moment. We have post-graduate degreed people that will not accept a client for counseling because their voting record causes them to fear for their safety. What neural pathways were built up in their brains? Who helped to build them?

The second very concerning issue that we discussed in our conversation was about trauma-informed care. Christine told me that students of psychology are now learning that instead of helping clients work through their trauma and then assisting them to build up resilience, they should just stop before getting to the resilience bit. It would be difficult not to see oneself as a perpetual victim without some modicum of resilience to rely upon—especially as it relates to a traumatic experience. School employees [207] are being trained to practice 'trauma-informed education.'[208] Similar to the instruction clinical psychology students are receiving, educators and school staff are being

[207] Portell, M. (2019, December 16). *Understanding trauma-informed education.* Edutopia. Retrieved on 2021 December 11: https://www.edutopia.org/article/understanding-trauma-informed-education.

[208] Venet, A. S. (2018 August 3). *The how and why of trauma-informed teaching.* Edutopia. Retrieved on 2021 December 11: https://www.edutopia.org/article/how-and-why-trauma-informed-teaching.

trained to recognize, but not actually do anything that's helpful. Instead, they treat 'restlessness,' 'distraction,' and other 'challenging behaviors' as evidence of trauma. There's absolutely no way that restless or angry kids who are expected to hold still in one place for hours on end might need more physical activity or hands-on work. Of course, there are children that have experienced trauma, and continue to because of their home situations. You'd have to be ignorant or unfeeling to assert anything different. The problem with associating restlessness or sudden outbursts with trauma is that it's a recipe for overdiagnosis. Teachers and other school staff have virtually no training in the field of psychology. Sefein noted that trauma-informed care is a specialty within psychology that typically requires additional time and training beyond standard requirements. Why should anyone expect that K-12 educators be able to ably practice trauma-informed teaching? We shouldn't.

Postmodernists and Critical Theorists have popularized 'standpoint epistemology' which, by design, eschews and undermines culture and its building-block meta-narratives. When society can't enforce norms, shared culture deteriorates. When culture is erased, society—as such—is no more. "But, culture and norms are oppression!"[209] False. Oppression can be

---

[209] O'Brien, E. (2004). *I Could Hear You If You Would Just Calm Down: Challenging Eurocentric Classroom Norms through Passionate Discussions of Racial Oppression. Counterpoints, 273*, 68-86. Retrieved on 2021 May 22: http://www.jstor.org/stable/42978603.

perpetuated by norms and culture. But, the existence of a culture does not presuppose oppression.

On July 15, 2020, news broke that the National Museum of African American History and Culture in Washington, D.C. had published a graphic to its website that asserted that ideals like "planning for the future," "punctuality," "being polite," and "the nuclear family," are simply manifestations of "white culture."

ASPECTS & ASSUMPTIONS OF WHITENESS
& WHITE CULTURE IN THE UNITED STATES

White dominant culture, or **whiteness**, refers to the ways white people and their traditions, attitudes and ways of life have been normalized over time and are now considered standard practices in the United States. And since white people still hold most of the institutional power in America, we have all internalized some aspects of white culture — including people of color.

Rugged Individualism
- The individual is the primary unit • Self-reliance
- Independence & autonomy highly valued + rewarded
- Individuals assumed to be in control of their environment, *"You get what you deserve"*

Family Structure
- The nuclear family: father, mother, 2.3 children is the ideal social unit
- Husband is breadwinner and head of household
- Wife is homemaker and subordinate to the husband
- Children should have own rooms, be independent

Emphasis on Scientific Method
- Objective, rational linear thinking
- Cause and effect relationships
- Quantitative emphasis

History
- Based on Northern European immigrants' experience in the United States
- Heavy focus on the British Empire
- The primacy of Western (Greek, Roman) and Judeo-Christian tradition

Protestant Work Ethic
- Hard work is the key to success
- Work before play
- "If you didn't meet your goals, you didn't work hard enough"

Religion
- Christianity is the norm
- Anything other than Judeo – Christian tradition is foreign
- No tolerance for deviation from single god concept

Status, Power & Authority
- Wealth = worth
- Your job is who you are
- Respect authority
- Heavy value on ownership of goods, space, property

Future Orientation
- Plan for future
- Delayed gratification
- Progress is always best
- "Tomorrow will be better"

Time
- Follow rigid time schedules
- Time viewed as a commodity

Aesthetics
- Based on European culture • Steak and potatoes; "bland is best"
- Woman's beauty based on blonde, thin – "Barbie"
- Man's attractiveness based on economic status, power, intellect

Holidays
- Based on Christian religions
- Based on white history & male leaders

Justice
- Based on English common law
- Protect property & entitlements
- Intent counts

Competition
- Be #1
- Win at all costs
- Winner/loser dichotomy
- Action Orientation
- Master and control nature
- Must always "do something" about a situation
- Aggressiveness and Extroversion
- Decision-Making
- Majority rules (when Whites have power)

Communication
- "The King's English" rules
- Written tradition
- Avoid conflict, intimacy
- Don't show emotion
- Don't discuss personal life
- Be polite

133

Within two days the graphic had been removed and the museum apologized for posting it on their website: "We erred in including the chart. We have removed it and we apologize." They noted, however, that they were glad to have sparked conversation about 'race.'[210]

This exercise provided one or two writers alongside one or two graphic designers with work for their wages. It also served to grossly misattribute a long list of ideals to people's culture that is purportedly shared simply based on the amount of melanin in their skin. Culture doesn't depend on melanin. To the ideologue, this doesn't matter. For the critical theorist, only power matters—and if the result of their words is that power is transferred from the oppressor to the oppressed, the effort was a success. Even if they have to hypersimplify actions or data to expose alleged inequities, or oppression, they'll do it to further the cause.[211] Collateral damage—to people or ideals—is expected, and sometimes even desired. Machiavelli would be proud.

---

[210] Koop, C., (2020 July 17). *Smithsonian museum apologizes for saying hard work, rational thought is 'white culture'.* Miami Herald.
[211] Peterson, J.B., (2021). *Beyond order: 12 more rules for life.* Random House. New York.

Other ways of knowing

When I was a kid in the 1980s and 90s, I remember hearing a time or two the phrase "moral relativism." The term had a decidedly negative connotation back then. It was largely dismissed as 'crazy' and 'fringe.' I don't believe I've heard it said more than a couple of times since the mid-90s. Part of the reason, I think, is that it's been replaced by other terms like 'other ways of knowing,' 'indigenous ways of knowing,' and 'cultural relativism.' The first two terms deal with the idea of reality as such and the third questions whether we should be able to judge reality (including others' actions). All three strike at the root of modern Western society and culture where reality is based on an inherent universal value structure that operates within a large and growing set of observable, testable facts.

Because there is no knowable reality, everything is relative—everything is fair game. You might 'know' something because of empirical data. But I could 'know' just the opposite because there are 'other ways of knowing.' From *New Discourses* (emphasis in original):

> *"Ways of knowing of interest to the Theory and activism of Critical Social Justice specifically include those that they deem to have been unjustly excluded or marginalized. These include tradition, superstition, storytelling, and emotion. They are considered to have been excluded by white, Western men who established their own (typically Eurocentric, white, and/or masculinist) ways of knowing—like science, reason, logic, and*

135

empiricism (see also, master's tools). Because white, Western men had the power to do so, they have unfairly privileged these approaches and imposed them upon other cultures (see also, colonialism)."[212]

One can immediately see the immense problems that can be created from such an anti-intellectual, anti-realism view. Worse still, some proponents of 'standpoint epistemology' insist that theirs is not the responsibility to explain or educate anyone about how they know what they do—presumably because they're a minority. However, members of the majority or dominant group are expected to learn and perpetuate the 'knowledges' of non-dominant groups:

"We suggest that researchers should try to bring Indigenous and Western approaches to knowledge creation into conversation, or link them for joint purposes, rather than trying to integrate them into one entity. To address power imbalances and philosophical differences, Western researchers must seek to learn about, preserve and build upon Indigenous knowledges and ways of knowing."[213]

---

[212] Lindsay, J., (2020, July 13). Ways of knowing. Translations from the wokish. New Discourses. Retrieved on 2021 April 14: https://newdiscourses.com/tftw-ways-of-knowing/

[213] Canadian Research Institute for the Advancement of Women. (n.d.). *What are indigenous and western ways of knowing?* CRIAW. Retrieved on 2021 May 22: https://www.criaw-icref.ca/images/userfiles/files/Fact%20Sheet%202%20EN%20FINAL.pdf.

Standpoint epistemology is simply a fancy way of saying, "I get to claim anything that suits me and If you disagree, you're ignorant and/or bigoted. From my perspective, this is true and if you try to convince me otherwise, or even doubt me, you're bad." What about those of us who respect the traditions and cultures of indigenous peoples and simultaneously value the benefits of Western medicine, technologies, etc.? We run the risk of being labeled as bigots by those who require not just respect and tolerance, but also celebration. Increasingly, loud voices in the Western world are publicly supportive of this type of subjectivism. We have large populations of people now who genuinely categorize disagreement as 'harm,' and 'violence.'

My lived experience

Closely related to standpoint epistemology is the ascription of quasi-empirical value to one individual's 'lived experience.' It also goes by another name, 'experiential knowledge.' Whichever way you choose to say it, it's anti-intellectual. Am I trying to discount personal experience and the value we can (and do) all gain from it? Of course not. What I am saying, however, is that one person's experience is no replacement for objective research and study. Critical theorists, postmodernists, and the rest of the neo-Kantians will, of course, take issue with this. But, that is to be expected.

"focusing on propositional knowledge… is itself a form of epistemic injustice. Such a focus neglects epistemic resources that help oppressed people craft more just worlds."[214]

There are several assumptions in the foregoing quote that are revealing. First, the usage of the word 'oppressed' is a cue to look for further evidence in the writing of the quintessential Marxian framing of oppressor and oppressed. We don't have to exercise much patience in the search for another clue—it's at the end of the same sentence. The assertion that only oppressed people have the power to end their oppression harks back to Freire (as mentioned in Chapter 5) and beyond him, back to Karl Marx himself. Next, there seems to be a pervasive disdain for underprivileged people among critical theorists and postmodernists, indeed among Marxists. Here, the writer removes even the capability of 'oppressed people' acquiring empirical knowledge. The woke are always looking for groups of people who need a benevolent overlord—a job title they see themselves as uniquely qualified to fill. Here we find another paradox of Wokeism: *"Only the oppressed have the power to free themselves. But, they're not intelligent or motivated enough to liberate themselves, so we will create an aristocracy to oversee their release from oppression."* Fortunately for the wokesters, they're not limited by the ridiculous and arbitrary constraints of logic and reason.

---

[214] Shotwell, A. (2017). *Forms of knowing and epistemic resources*. The Routledge Handbook of Epistemic Injustice. Routledge.

The concept of 'lived experience' as a useful tool in the interpretation and understanding of the world, of reality itself, owes in large part to the work of Edmund Husserl.[215] Husserl and others after him built a body of work that is now referred to as phenomenology. One of his personal assistants, Martin Heidegger, whose name you'll recognize from the chapter on Critical Theory (Chapter 3), continued the study of 'the structures of personal experience.' That philosophers studied how people experience reality isn't so surprising or interesting. What is interesting is the extent to which this concept has been grown and warped to encroach on the importance and validity of objective reality. It's been allowed to do so because it serves, at the very least, a political purpose. People's personal feelings, their 'lived experiences,' are reason enough to change rules, regulations, laws, and policies. The field of legal study that started as 'legal realism' which then became 'critical legal studies'—and served as the jumping off point for Derrick Bell's 'critical race theory'—asserts that laws are flexible and meant to change over time to accurately address the 'changing needs of society,' What better way to bend legal structures in your favor—when empiricism isn't getting the job done—than to appeal to arbitrary, but effective, 'lived experience?' And, here we are.

---

[215] SEP. (2013 December 16). *Phenomenology*. Stanford Encyclopedia of Philosophy. Retrieved on 2021 June 8: https://plato.stanford.edu/entries/phenomenology/.

Chapter 10 | Activist Teacher Colleges

"...the schools of education served as handmaidens to the public school system: they trained teachers and administrators, as well as serving as high-level consultants for the operation of the system."[216]

In a country with a long and storied history of run-ins with the Establishment Clause, many of our fellow Americans seem quite willing to establish woke ideologies as the state religion where K-12 schools are their chapels and colleges and universities are their seminaries. Having said that, Wokeism doesn't map perfectly onto religion because religious thinkers and philosophers have, for centuries, applied rigor to their ideas and been willing to engage in debate about those ideas. Those within the discipline have proven entirely unwilling to apply that same rigor. When critics make the attempt to do so from without, they're instantly denounced as bigots, chauvinists, or racists.

One of the major benefits—to the committed ideologue—of replacing analytical philosophy, or critical thinking, with procedural training in university education departments[217] (where

---

[216] Waddington, D., (2020). *The importance of philosophy in teacher education.* Routledge. New York. (25-44).
[217] Barrow, R. (2020). *The importance of philosophy in teacher education.* Routledge. New York. (15-24).

aspiring teachers get their degrees) is that the higher-level thinking is already done. They avoid rigorous thought and debate. No analysis or critical thinking needed.

'Just present this material in this way for this kind of student, and in that way for that kind. '

'Adhere to these policies in this way.'

'Comply with this regulation and report your compliance on this schedule. '

When the focus moves from philosophy and principle to procedure and practice, the connection learners have to the 'why' can quickly evaporate. And, in that circumstance, conditions are ideal for a drift from any kind of tradition—whether philosophical or practical. This is what has happened. Teachers-in-training are no longer asked to think any more deeply than absolutely necessary. Instead of being equipped with the logical and rhetorical skills needed to consider and debate a variety of pedagogies, they are simply handed the 'right ones' by their professors.

This is unlikely to change for as long as there exists a mutually beneficial and powerful relationship between schools of education and the K-12 public schooling system—with one caveat: there must also remain intact a third element, that of dependence. Teacher colleges in the West are necessarily dependent on other fields of study. This shouldn't be all that surprising, given that a K-12 teacher's job is to pass along knowledge to children in several different disciplines, rather than to come up with new knowledge as such. Their dependence is deepened and perpetuated by the fact that they have no periodic tables, complex theorems, or laws (of physics). In order to fit in with their colleagues in other departments, they cling to outmoded, inefficient, and ineffective ideas. For example, schools of education tend to lionize the ideas of John Dewey, perhaps in part simply to benefit through association with his name and popularity. However, that strategy may be doomed to failure should his popularity decline.[218]

John Dewey was renowned in his own time for his philosophy of education. He popularized 'experiential learning' and was among the elite group of early 20th century progressives who had extensive influence among policymakers and academics alike. Dewey believed, as a constructionist, that you could—indeed that you should—remake society by educating children in such a way that a some-day-utopia could be achieved. Dewey wanted to reconstruct society by adjusting "individual activity on the basis of social consciousness," which was, for him, the only "sure method of social reconstruction."[219] Charles Sanders Peirce, one of his instructors at Johns Hopkins University, had studied

---

[218] Waddington, D. (2020).
[219] Dewey, J. (1897). *My pedagogic creed.* School Journal. 54(77-80).

Kant's *Critique of Pure Reason* deeply, though he ultimately eschewed significant portions of his philosophy in favor of pragmatism. Like many among the intelligentsia in his time, he believed that he had the proper vision for the future of society at large and that he could contribute to the realization of that desirable future state by molding children in their youth to become 'contributing members of society.' Mind you, Dewey's definitions of these words likely don't match your definitions.

Is it any surprise, then, that we hear about teachers across the country reenacting the selling of slaves at early American slave markets with small children play-acting the various roles? Or, that the Holocaust is simulated in a school play? It happens— even today.[220] Dewey is a legend among professors of education and they continue to teach that children learn best by role playing. Until teachers are trained to steer away from these kinds of learning activities, there will always be a risk that students are required to participate in something that is not just inappropriate, but potentially psychologically harmful. To be clear, I'm not suggesting that role-playing or hands-on activities are ineffective methods of teaching. Obviously, they can be of great value instructional tools. However, these methods combined with activist teaching make for very eye-catching news headlines. Worse than the headlines, children are sometimes acting out truly

---

[220] Onion, R. (2019 20 May). *What it felt like.* Slate. Retrieved on 2021 May 18: https://slate.com/human-interest/2019/05/history-classroom-role-playing-games-slavery-holocaust.html

horrific events at the direction of one of the primary authority figures in their young lives—their teachers. This is unconscionable, and it's happening because activist teachers are indoctrinated by activist professors during an impressionable time in their lives when many of them are living on their own for the first time, away from home. The selection of a university can no longer consist of enrolling in the highest ranked school to which the student applied—if it ever could have. Students and parents cannot afford to forego researching the campus culture and climate. Campus tours should include thorough research on what Diversity, Inclusion, and Equity initiatives are being implemented and the effect they're having on student life. Parents and students would benefit from a rating or ranking system of colleges and universities that specifically measures levels of 'wokeness.' This may consider the number of professors with 'critical theory,' 'critical race theory,' 'critical pedagogy,' or 'postmodernism' listed among their interests or areas of research. Another consideration might be how many times the words 'diversity,' 'inclusion,' and 'equity' make appearances on the schools' websites, etc.

In the meantime, students continue to enroll in classes at K-12 schools, colleges, and universities where their teachers,[221]

---

[221] Latour, K. (2018 March 21). *I'm proud of my students and their courageous activism.* American Federation of Teachers. Retrieved on 2021 June 7: https://aftvoices.org/im-proud-of-my-students-and-their-courageous-activism-2cb8b83ec568.

professors, and administrators[222] are proud of the fact that they're training activists and ideologues.

Headlines like '*Activism is Good Teaching,*' and '*More Students Are Becoming Activists. Teachers Can Help Strengthen Their Voice,*' are commonplace today. In a 2018 study, "*school counselors at secondary schools were asked to indicate how the current intensity of political rhetoric has affected students in their schools.*"[223] 52% of the counselors polled indicated that students had increased their own activism as a result. It seems reasonable to infer that some portion of those students who took more of an interest in activist causes were influenced by activist teachers—adults with whom they spend upwards of seven hours each weekday. We have many examples of teachers complaining about and/or celebrating political events to their students. A quick internet search will turn up dozens of such news stories just in the past few years.

One teacher who believes that there are few reasonable boundaries between activism and teaching explains that it is one of the primary functions of a teacher to provide "…*written feedback that highlights the flaws in a student's evidence,*

---

[222] Kim, Y. (2021 April 6). *Chief Diversity Officer Robin Means Coleman discusses student activism, vision for equity, and demands.* The Daily Northwestern. Retrieved on 2021 June 7: https://dailynorthwestern.com/2021/04/06/campus/chief-diversity-officer-robin-means-coleman-discusses-student-activism-vision-for-equity-and-demands/.

[223] NACAC. (2018). *Effects of political rhetoric on college-bound students.* National Association for College Admission Counseling. (3).

reasoning, or perspective on moral, religious, or political issues;" For some parents and children, this perspective may be perfectly acceptable—likely dependent on the degree to which the views of both parties are aligned. For everyone else in the class, this poses a serious problem. The space between what the teacher and parents feel is the role of the teacher is a breeding ground for conflict.

Jessica Chamness, an aspiring teacher quoted in a National Education Association article titled *Student Activism on the Rise*, said, '*I just want to open [students'] eyes. I think that if they see the mistakes we have made and the terrible positions we have taken, and then learn about other cultures, they will take another step forward...*'[224] The same article notes that activism isn't new to teachers and aspiring teachers:

> "*Educators, and especially young educators, have always gravitated toward activism. But young people are more engaged now than they have been in generations, and they are active in a wide array of issues. They took action throughout the presidential election and were considerably more likely to vote than in previous years. They may even have played a key role in Joe Biden's victory.*"

---

[224] Paterson, J. (2021 March 9). Student activism on the rise. National Education Association. Retrieved on 2021 June 7: https://www.nea.org/advocating-for-change/new-from-nea/student-activism-rise.

What does wokeness in teacher colleges look like? Let's consider the following examples. One of the most highly-regarded and well-known teacher colleges is at Columbia University.

From their website:

The Office for Diversity and Community Affairs was created in January 2001, in response to recommendations of the President's 1999 Taskforce Report. The Office for Diversity and Community Affairs leads the President's and College's initiatives concerning community, diversity, civility, equity, and anti-discrimination. The Office, working with others in the College, addresses issues from faculty, staff, students, and alumni. These concerns may overlap with equity, anti-discrimination, retaliation and due process concerns, sexual assault and other gender-based misconduct concerns. The philosophy is to encourage the College community to listen, learn, educate, and work together in positive ways. At the same time, the Office focuses on systemic issues by addressing policy and procedural concerns.[225]

One assistant professor at Arizona State University lists among her areas of expertise, "Feminist Theory," "Social Justice in Education," and "Critical Race Theory."

---

[225] https://www.tc.columbia.edu/diversity/

Assistant Professor Carrie Sampson teaches at the Mary Lou Fulton Teachers College at ASU in Tempe, Arizona. In the Spring of 2021, five of the six courses[226] she was responsible to teach were limited to her own research—or that of her students—ensuring that K-12 schools will continue to be examined by, and receive prescriptions from, people rich in degrees, yet poor in useful information or solutions.

Expertise Areas

Feminist Theory

Local Community Influence

Bilingual and English Language Learners

Educational Leadership and Administration

Educational Policy and Politics

Race and Racism in Education

Social Justice in Education

Critical Race Theory

Another professor, Dr. Sarah Diem (University of Missouri College of Education; Columbia, Missouri) has authored and co-authored several studies on diversity, equity, antiracism, and inclusion. The abstract from a study in 2018 reads:

"In this study, we examined how graduate students in a leadership preparation program developed their racially aware identities while professionally embedded in a district that utilizes school choice policies and practices. Our findings illustrate the intentional work necessary to develop school leaders with antiracist identities."[227]

---

[226] https://education.asu.edu/about/people/carrie-sampson
[227] *Diem, S., Carpenter, B. W., & Lewis-Durham, T. (2019). Preparing Antiracist School Leaders in a School Choice Context. Urban*

148

University of Delaware (2004)[228]

New graduates come out of their training with a set of presumptions passed on to them from their trainers. When the entire syllabus for each course is undeniably Marxian and constructivist, you can be confident in your choice to turn down any offers to attend that school.

For any who may be skeptical that these ideas have actually gained any significant hold in schools of education, five minutes spent on a simple internet search will convince you otherwise. For instance, Stanford University offers a graduate degree to educators that includes a required course on 'Building Classroom

---

[228]
Education, 54(5), 706–731. https://doi.org/10.1177/0042085918783812

https://docs.google.com/viewerng/viewer?url=https://ctal.udel.edu/files/2019/07/MCA-final-report-for-website.pdf&hl=en

Communities.' The course description reads, in part, '…*young people are taught academic content that can be drilled and tested rather than understanding literacies and numeracies as forms of power…*"[229]

Another useful and informative exercise is to count the number of professors at a given school that have research interests in woke ideologies like 'critical race theory,' 'critical women's studies,' 'equity,' etc. You may consider looking up the faculty at your local college or university and determining the proportion of overtly woke professors to the total number of professors. You can learn a lot about an institution and their ideological commitments in this way.

---

[229] Stanford University. (n.d.). *Stanford Teacher Education Program.* Retrieved on 2021 June 7: https://ed.stanford.edu/step/academics/elementary/curriculum-outline.

Chapter 11 | The DIE Triad

What explains the fact that over 80% of professional basketball players are Black, as are about 70% of professional football players? Only an idiot would chalk it up to diversity and inclusion.
Instead, it is excellence that explains the disproportionate numbers.
Jewish Americans, who are just 3% of our population, win over 35% of the Nobel prizes in science that are awarded to Americans. Again, it is excellence that explains the disproportionality, not diversity and inclusion.[230]

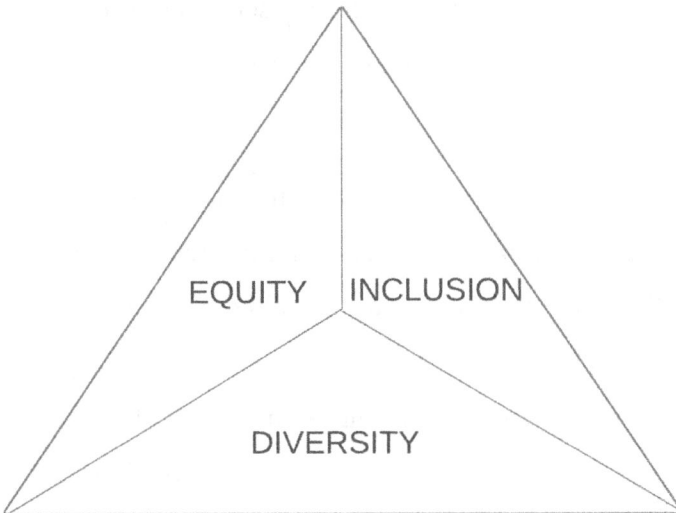

EQUITY   INCLUSION

DIVERSITY

---

[230] Williams, W. (2020 September 2). *Diversity, equity, and inclusion nonsense.* Walter E. Williams. Retrieved on 2021 May 27: http://walterewilliams.com/diversity,-equity-and-inclusion-nonsense/.

The triad of wokeness: diversity, inclusion, and equity, each sound like they're universally desirable values to pursue—even for the non-religious.

Why would anyone with even a semblance of moral character want anything less than an inclusive school, or workplace? Similarly, you'd have to be outright racist or sexist if you oppose diversity, right? And, equity would only be opposed by the greedy privileged who will stop at nothing to hoard resources. The words used to describe these ideals are well-known and they have positive connotations. Why do you hate and fight against the universal "Good?" This is the framing, the vantage point, that's been concocted around the 'DIE triad,' and to oppose any of them—for any reason whatsoever—is more than shortsighted or ignorant, it's heretical. A heretic eschews religious tradition or principles, making it an apt analog to *Wokeism* as a quasi-religious worldview.

While many of us believe that we can, should, and do support diversity, inclusion, and equity, it's important to take a closer look. It's particularly important for citizens to understand what is really meant by these words when they're used as titles or in descriptions of activities, trainings, and curricula intended for use within schools. There is a very high likelihood that your local school district has adopted and implemented a program in the past few years that is intended to increase *diversity, inclusion,* and *equity* (DIE). The remainder of this chapter will explore each element of the DIE triad and attempt to show that these three noble nouns are often being misused—resulting in widespread misunderstandings of what is actually being taught in schools.

> *"Popular perception can overwhelm truth and accuracy in establishing a communication connection... words that had certain definitions when your grandparents were your age may have an entirely different meaning today."*[231]

Diversity isn't what you think it is.

> *"...[diversity] aims to privilege the marginalized and marginalize the privileged in order to redress the imbalances it sees in society..."*[232]

Diversity, as an ideal, has enjoyed decades of status as a virtuous aspiration in a wide array of settings (academia, business, education, government, etc.). However, it's unclear what diversity actually gains anybody. This isn't to say that homogeneity is preferable to diversity, per se. But, this misses the point. The word 'diversity' has become "almost magical" and every time we hear it, we begin to drool "like Pavlov's dogs."[233] And, besides, what does it mean? Diversity of viewpoints is

---

[231] Luntz, F. (2007). *Words that work. It's not what you say, it's what people hear.* Hyperion. New York. *49-50.*

[232] Lindsay, J., (2020, July 13). Diversity. Translations from the wokish. New Discourses. Retrieved on 2021 April 14: https://newdiscourses.com/tftw-equity/

[233] Sowell, T. (1995, September 15). *Thomas Sowell* [Video]. Charlie Rose. https://charlierose.com/videos/16711.

something that is worth a serious conversation, whereas diversity based solely on melanin levels seems unlikely to yield any significant benefits—and may actually lead to harm. People much more intelligent than me have pointed out that 'diversity' in many elite university undergraduate classes amounts to almost completely homogenous groups of people, but for skin pigmentation. They live in the same neighborhoods, their parents work at the same organizations, their household incomes are virtually identical. So, is variation in skin tone the real goal of diversity initiatives? Since every individual is unique, by definition, you increase the diversity of any group simply by adding another person.

The history of diversity as a goal for education and the American workforce in the United States goes back at least to 1987 with the release of a Hudson Institute study that was commissioned by the U.S. Department of Labor. The 117-page study is titled *Workforce 2000*.[234] While the authors of the study don't overtly advocate for proportional quantities of workers in each sector of the economy, they very clearly state repeatedly that an increasingly diverse working population will need to be educated and employed in the U.S. This study has been cited over 2,950 times since it was written. A large number of those citations come from research articles which advocate for increased diversity—for its own sake.

---

[234] Johnston, W.B., et al. (1987). Workforce 2000.

If diversity is what we're after, but we can't define it or can't explain what benefits are supposedly derived by its achievement, should we be adding it to our mission statements or public declarations? A New York Times Magazine's Walter Benn Michaels echoed a familiar sentiment about what efforts for diversity actually result in: *"When student and faculty activists struggle for campus cultural diversity, they are in large part battling over what skin color rich kids should have."*[235] There's no arguing with this. This is exactly what happens in practice.

In practical terms, the real question parents should be asking is something like, "How will your efforts to 'increase diversity' impact my child, my child's relationship with friends who don't look like them, the classroom, the school, and our community?" Parents who can verify that the impact of 'increasing diversity' will simply be that their child and her classmates will be more caring and accepting of others, ought to count themselves fortunate for having dodged the negative outcomes of virtually all diversity programs wherever they're taught. K-12 classrooms are no exception. Whether it's a diversity training for teachers and staff, or a training session on increasing diversity in hiring, such efforts have a long history[236] of simply failing. And, more

---

[235] Michaels, W.B . (2004 April 25). *Diversity's false solace.* New York Times Magazine. Retrieved on 2021 May 27: https://www.nytimes.com/2004/04/25/magazine/l-diversity-s-false-solace-334480.html.

[236] Dishman, L. (2018, August 4). A brief history of diversity training. Fast Company. Retrieved on 2021 May 19:

than failing,[237] these sessions very often result in the opposite of what was intended.

Let's look at some examples of what this looks like in practice.

In November of 2018, the Noblesville, Indiana school board held a meeting to discuss diversity training that would be implemented in the wake of the discovery of some offensive and racist messages written by a student in a school bathroom. The first session of the training had been completed one day prior, a portion of which required that students be separated into groups based on their skin color for breakout sessions. One parent commented on the practice,

"That's not how you engage a student, by separating them and reminding them that they're different," [Kathryn] Ehrgott said. "You get them together and you talk. You have a conversation."[238]

https://www.fastcompany.com/40579246/a-brief-history-of-diversity-training.

[237] Thomas, R. R. (1990). From affirmative action to affirming diversity. Harvard Business Review. Retrieved on 2021 May 19: https://hbr.org/1990/03/from-affirmative-action-to-affirming-diversity.

[238] McClellan, M. (2018, November 21). Diversity training at Noblesville high school upsets some parents. WRTV. Retrieved on 2021 May 19: https://www.wrtv.com/news/local-news/hamilton-county/diversity-training-at-noblesville-high-school-upsets-some-parents.

The next example comes from New York City in 2019 when then-Commissioner Richard Carranza announced an overhaul of the curriculum for the city's schools.[239] This new curriculum "seeks to enhance student "consciousness" in varying ways, from outlining racial privilege hierarchies to emphasizing a more diverse array of historical figures and events." Of course, a widened view of historical figures to include in instruction seems perfectly harmless. Racial privilege hierarchies, however, are extremely unlikely to improve relations between students, faculty, and staff. They're also strictly speculative.

The final example comes from Southlake, Texas, where in 2020, Kathy Del Calvo stood in a school board meeting to say, "What I cannot accept is that these ideologies are being forced on my grandchildren. They are all minorities. They do not need to be treated special. They can stand on their own. Their race and ethnicity means nothing. We've taught them that hard work will get them everywhere."[240] Del Calvo was objecting to the district's then-proposed Cultural Competence Action

[239] Algar, S. (2019, September 23). *DOE's curricular diversity overhaul slated to begin this year*. New York Post. Retrieved on 2021 May 19: https://nypost.com/2019/09/23/does-curricular-diversity-overhaul-slated-to-begin-this-year/.
[240] Campbell, E. (2020, August 17). Parents protest Carroll schools' diversity plan, saying it promotes 'reverse racism'. Ft. Worth Star-Telegram.

Plan—a plan that called for the integration of "diversity and inclusion training for students" into daily curriculum and lessons.

Inclusion isn't what you think it is.

"[Inclusion] means to create a welcoming environment specifically for groups considered marginalized, and this entails the exclusion of anything that could feel unwelcoming to any identity groups... This is because everything in Critical Social Justice must be understood in terms of systemic power dynamics that it Theorizes characterize all of social, if not material, reality."[241]

Absolute inclusion requires a complete absence of so-called 'microaggressions.' According to Dr. Derald Sue, microaggressions are "...communicative, somatic, environmental or relational cues that demean and/or disempower members of minority groups in virtue of their minority status."[242] In other words, they are social slights. They're words or actions that demonstrate mild (usually unconscious) contempt for another person. But, arguments about how to solve the ever-widening problem of microaggressions rings hollow when you come to learn of a disturbing "...lack of reliable data about the prevalence and harm of microaggressions..."[243]

---

[241] Lindsay, J., (2020, July 13). Inclusion. Translations from the wokish. New Discourses. Retrieved on 2021 April 15: https://newdiscourses.com/tftw-inclusion/

[242] Al-Gharbi, M., (2017). The big debate about microaggressions. Retrieved on 2021 April 15: https://musaalgharbi.com/2017/01/30/big-debate-microaggressions/

[243] AL-Gharbi, M., (2017).

Inclusion can only be accomplished with the help of individuals who *"occupy dominant identity categories and/or positions of leadership and privilege."*[244] To be clear, however, if an individual in a position of leadership is themselves a minority, no one expects them to be particularly 'inclusive' of anyone else. And, as it turns out, 'inclusivity by powerful people from marginalized groups,' can be as difficult to find as it's purported to be by people from 'dominant' groups.[245]

The ideal of inclusion calls on people with power to 'elevate' and 'amplify' the voices of people of color (POCs). The premise behind this expectation is that once amplified, the voices of historically marginalized peoples will be (1) heard and (2) heeded, which will result in (3) policy changes that (4) lift the oppressed out of their oppression. It's been said many times before in language much more elegant than I can muster, but our world's societies have provided us with precious few examples of marginalized groups who gained significant political power, which they then leveraged into economic prosperity relative to dominant groups. Typically, the order is reversed.[246]

---

[244] AWIS. (2019 October 3). *Creating inclusive spaces: A how-to for change makers and allies.* Association for Women in Science. Retrieved on 2021 May 27: https://www.awis.org/inclusive-spaces/.

[245] Glaser, A. (2020 May 13). *Current and ex-employees allege Google drastically rolled back diversity and inclusion programs.* NBC News. Retrieved on 2021 May 27: https://www.nbcnews.com/news/us-news/current-ex-employees-allege-google-drastically-rolled-back-diversity-inclusion-n1206181.

[246] Sowell, T. (1983). *The Economics and Politics of Race.* William Morrow.

Of course, it goes without saying that no reasonable or caring person would argue against including people, and particularly those who need assistance most. Worldwide religions are based on this ideal. Though, there is a stark contrast between the motivation of a religious believer attempting to follow the example of their deity through service, or lifting others up, and the activist who announces their beneficence on every social media channel available to them to signal their virtue. One recognizes empowering the powerless as an inherent moral good. The other is looking for validation and notoriety.

Equity isn't what you think it is.

"Where equality means that citizen A and citizen B are treated equally, equity means "adjusting shares in order to make citizens A and B equal." In that sense, equity is something like a kind of "social communism,"...the intentional redistribution of shares, but not necessarily along lines of existing economic disparity but in order to adjust for and correct current and historical injustices, both as exist in reality and as have been drawn out by the various critical theories."[247]

Like the other two components of the DIE triad, equity sure sounds nice. We're told that if only we could all work together to usher in equity, we'd be 33.3% of the way to our new utopia. The other 66.6% will be accomplished with the adoption of

---

[247] Lindsay, J., (2020, July 13). Equity. Translations from the wokish. New Discourses. Retrieved on 2021 April 14: https://newdiscourses.com/tftw-equity/

appropriate systemic implementations of diversity and inclusion, of course.

In order for equity to truly be achieved, guilt must first be confessed by the current or historic oppressors, or their progeny. Bear in mind that whether the progeny of oppressors knowingly perpetuate historic oppression on any other groups makes absolutely no difference. From the vantage point of the Marxian theorist, all systems currently in place right now in the Western world uphold and sustain oppression. To deny this is merely a symptom of 'White Fragility' (if you're 'white-presenting,' i.e. you look white), or it's internalized white supremacy for everyone else. For both sets of people, deprogramming is the only way out. If you've heard anything about re-education camps for conservatives, libertarians, and moderate Democrats, this is what you'd be re-educated into. Everyone must believe in wokeness and adhere to the new orthodoxy or suffer the consequences.

In order to truly achieve equity for everyone, we must measure and gauge each individual's current circumstances relative to the most advantaged person in society. Then, we redistribute resources among everyone until every single person has the exact same amount of everything—*everything*. Not just access to education, but education. Not just opportunities for a good job, but employment. Not just equality of opportunity, but equality of outcomes. Not just equality, but equity.

There's at least one problem with this, and it comes from within the ideological framework of the Marxian theorists who advocate for this ideal. Equity is unachievable because measurements can not be taken at the individual level. Every person's group identities are more important than their individual characteristics. The fact that 'black people aren't a monolith,' 'Asian people aren't all the same,' and 'non-white Hispanics are individually unique' is irreconcilable with Marxian framing. As a result, equity is only ever possible at the group level—and, even then, only in theory.

If this definition and explanation doesn't sound very appealing or beneficial, that's because it's not. Pursuing equity as defined by the critical theorists actually does an immense amount of damage—to individuals' psyches, relationships, organizations, and societies. There are many examples provided in this book, and no doubt you've seen many more.

Chapter 12 | Curriculum Infused with Wokeness

They have recast the United States as an oppressor nation that must be deconstructed and subverted through politics. The curriculum's vision statement makes this aim explicit: it presents education not as a means of achieving competency, but as a "tool for transformation, social, economic, and political change, and liberation."[248]

It is from the 'woke seminaries' of America's institutions of higher education that K-12 curriculum emanates. But, the curriculum has to be adopted by somebody; just because you 'build it', that's no guarantee that 'they will come.' To anyone that has been paying attention, it should come as something less than a surprise that wokeness extends far beyond teacher colleges and curriculum publishers. The target market for these products and services is schools, of course. Schools throughout the West are hiring these teachers and purchasing these textbooks. The top administrators at school districts throughout America came up through those same colleges and universities. And, even the oldest among them are not old enough to have avoided the ideologies that continue to dominate the profession.

---

[248] Rufo, C.F. (2021 March 10). *Revenge of the gods*. City Journal. Retrieved on 2021 May 27: https://www.city-journal.org/calif-ethnic-studies-curriculum-accuses-christianity-of-theocide.

If those administrators weren't totally sold on wokeness personally, they'd nevertheless find it difficult to withstand the screeches coming from the wokesters—especially when their compensation packages carry promises of high-percentage retirement pensions. Longevity is key, so they largely 'go along to get along.' Deviation from the current push to infuse these ideologies could cost a superintendent or principal their jobs. There's nothing that can be said about the committed ideologue that signs purchase orders for woke curriculum. They're acting in accordance with their beliefs. What can we say about the skeptical school administrators that place those orders? They recognize that the textbooks they're directing faculty to use in the instruction of children may be harmful to children far beyond childhood. What of them? Public pressure can be extremely difficult to withstand—especially when you'd be fighting against the universal goods of 'inclusion,' 'social emotional learning,' and so on.

There are far too many examples of wokeness in schools to list here, let alone describe. An internet search for "antiracist" "school" "whiteness" will turn up plenty of reading material for those interested in understanding the scope of this issue.

In Seattle, math classes have taken a Marxist twist: they will "…encourage students to explore how math has been "appropriated" by Western culture and used in systems of power and oppression…"[249]

California's high school students will be required to complete a course in ethnic studies prior to graduation, beginning in the 2029-2030 school year. But, there's a catch: the selected curriculum for that course can *"Not teach or promote religious doctrine."*[250] Some might argue that ethnic studies is simply a secular religion. You might, therefore, ask whether the statute is internally consistent—a perfectly valid question.

In 2018, the Indiana Department of Education, after a mandate by the state's legislature, required that all high schools offer a semester-long course in ethnic studies[251]. The Department approved "Indiana Academic Standards Ethnic Studies" in June of the same year. The first among these standards (Standard 1.1) states,

> *"Students describe and defend the appropriate terminology including but not limited to race, ethnicity, culture, cultural practices, bias, **implicit bias**, and **critical consciousness**"*
> *(emphasis added).*

---

[249] Gewerz, C. (2019 October 14). Seattle schools lead controversial push to 'rehumanize' math. Retrieved on 2021 April 16: https://www.edweek.org/teaching-learning/seattle-schools-lead-controversial-push-to-rehumanize-math/2019/10. Education Week.

[250] California Education Code 51225.3 & 51226.7 (Amended January 31, 2019)

[251] https://www.doe.in.gov/news/indiana-department-education-announces-new-landmark-ethnic-studies-course-and-standards

A few pages later, standard 3.2:

"Students assess how social policies and economic forces offer privilege or systematic oppressions for racial/ethnic groups related to accessing social, political, and economic opportunities."

-Indiana Academic Standards Ethnic Studies (2018)

"A common feature of the classes is discussing how oppression and privilege shape one's group identity, whether white or black, straight or gay, male or female, binary or nonbinary, among the identity categories commonly recognized in the discipline."

Still, ethnic studies programs now enjoy a reach that was unimaginable when the movement was launched by a student coalition calling itself the Third World Liberation Front at San Francisco State University in 1968 with a five-month campus strike and demands to change the Eurocentric curriculum.

"One of the advances in the last 40-50 years is we are in the professoriate, administrative, faculty, superintendents of schools, we're now in the legislature," said Kenneth Monteiro, a professor of psychology at San Francisco State University and former dean of the College of Ethnic Studies. "We're just in a resurgence now."[252]

---

[252] https://www.realclearinvestigations.com/articles/2019/09/17/

woke_history_is_making_big_inroads_in_americas_high_schools_1 20363.html

Implicit Bias

Everyone has preferences. Everyone has biases. These two are not the same, except perhaps on their borders. Of course, the connotations of each word are very different. No one likes to admit they have biases, particularly when in reference to other people. Implicit bias is also sometimes referred to as 'unconscious bias.' Presumably, we're born with it or acculturated to it. Because it's unconscious, even if you wanted to admit to it and own it, you couldn't—not without help, that is.

How do you know if you have implicit bias—or how much of it? Two Harvard psychologists have devised an online test that, once completed, helps you to quantify just how biased you are. It's called the Implicit Association Test. Now, this might sound interesting, and maybe even helpful, if you're open to self-reflection and willing to put some effort into improving yourself for the benefit of others. There's just one problem, however: "…even the creators of the IAT cannot endorse it as a genuinely useful diagnostic instrument for individuals."[253] If this sounds like 21st century snake oil, that's because it might just be. At the very least, it's a procedural formality that allows organizations to

---

[253] Singal, J. (2021 April 9). *The false promise of quick-fix psychology.* Wall Street Journal. Retrieved on: 2021 April 16: https://www.wsj.com/articles/the-false-promise-of-quick-fix-psychology-11617981093.

claim they actually care about and value others when it indicates no such thing.

Decolonizing education

How can you 'decolonize' education?[254] Remove all positive references in curriculum to anyone who instigated or perpetuated oppression of any kind and increase the quantity and quality of references to the oppressed. This inverts the power dynamics currently in place, freeing the oppressed—yes, even if only in the curriculum. This is possible because power is derived from words. Language is what we use to construct reality, and the more of our language that is dedicated to raising up the oppressed, the more they are actually liberated. This is how it's purported to work, by Critical Theorists.

But, what if the problem isn't that curriculum is 'colonized?' What if we're taking our eyes off the ball when the real problem—where there is one—is that many Americans have instilled in their children a kind of 'friction with school?'[255] For instance, Prof. John McWhorter has maintained for over two decades that "Black students castigate the black student who

---

[254] Massey-Jones, R. (2019 May 21). *Why decolonizing education is important.* Sippin the EquiTEA. Retrieved on 2021 April 9: https://medium.com/@eec/why-decolonizing-education-is-important-77fc6b3e9085.
[255] McWhorter, J. (2000) *Losing the race. Self-sabotage in black America.* Free Press. New York. (145).

embraces school not simply as an attempt to "maintain cultural distinctiveness in contrast to the model of the oppressor" but out of a sense of insult."[256] *Hillbilly Elegy* elicits a similar dynamic among poor white communities. So, is there really a problem with a traditional curriculum that focuses primarily on core subjects with an eye toward the ultimate goal of proficiency in preparation for the workforce? Or, is that just exactly what we've abandoned in favor of a quasi-religious ideology that stirs up contention?

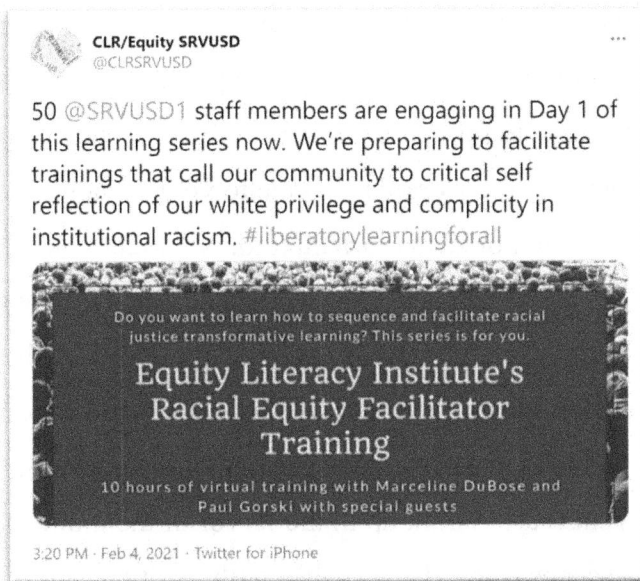

CLR/Equity SRVUSD
@CLRSRVUSD

50 @SRVUSD1 staff members are engaging in Day 1 of this learning series now. We're preparing to facilitate trainings that call our community to critical self reflection of our white privilege and complicity in institutional racism. #liberatorylearningforall

Do you want to learn how to sequence and facilitate racial justice transformative learning? This series is for you.

Equity Literacy Institute's Racial Equity Facilitator Training

10 hours of virtual training with Marceline DuBose and Paul Gorski with special guests

3:20 PM · Feb 4, 2021 · Twitter for iPhone

The San Ramon Valley Unified School District trains their staff on how they all contribute to white supremacy:[257] There is a series of tweets from this Twitter account around this same time

---

[256] *Ibid.* (148).
[257] SRVUSD. [@CLRSRVUSD]. (2021 February 4). https://twitter.com/CLRSRVUSD/status/1357453993513947137?s=2 0. [Tweet].

frame (February 2021) that announces to the world that San Ramon Valley USD school teachers are racist bigots that unwittingly—and sometimes wittingly—reinforce systems of oppression against their students in the classroom. This would be like your employer announcing on social media that everyone in your department at work is irredeemably prejudiced and that the only hope you have of maintaining any semblance of dignity is to complete this training—by an outside, paid consultant that you don't know. Then, and only then, will you wake up to the bigoted horrors that you perpetuate by your very existence. If you're a minority, you're likely to be publicly interrogated in an effort to bring to light examples of verbal violence you've experienced in the workplace—due to your melanin levels, gender identity, or sexual orientation. No doubt you've repressed memories that need to be exposed and atoned for by your coworkers. Where true harm has been done by prejudiced and bigoted individuals, recompense should be made. Of course. Too often, participants (those who choose not to simply zip their mouths shut) are caught up in the fervor of the moment and they reenact scenes from The Crucible. Silly isn't the right word for this kind of situation.

Buffalo, New York

On February 23, 2021, Christopher Rufo, award-winning independent filmmaker and writer, posted on X (@realchrisrufo) several images from Buffalo Public Schools (New York, USA) along with transcripts of a training provided to teachers and administrators by the school district:

"In kindergarten, teachers require students to watch a video that dramatizes dead black children warning them about the dangers of being killed by 'racist police and state-sanctioned violence.'"

He also wrote an article in City Journal that was published the same day:[258]

---

[258] Rufo, C. (2021 February 23). Failure factory. Retrieved on 2021 April 16: https://www.city-journal.org/buffalo-public-schools-critical-race-theory-curriculum

Rufo explains that the district's curriculum "…instruct[s] students that American society was designed for the "impoverishment of people of color and enrichment of white people…" Of course, as Rufo points out, in a district where only 18% of students are proficient in math and 20% in English, there are priorities higher on the list than the fundamental reshaping of the Western world. One has to wonder at the nerve of so-called educators who blame 'systems of oppression' for poor student achievement. Tragically, they'll likely get away with neglecting their duty to teach these children valuable knowledge and skills that would open new possibilities to them, simply because perpetuation of abject failure can easily be blamed on the kids, their families, and the neighborhoods. What would happen if the schools were turned over completely to a high-performing charter school network with a long track record of success? Let's hope we find out. Thousands of children will lead better lives if they're so fortunate.

Dedham, Massachusetts

In January of 2021, Dedham Public Schools officials, including the superintendent, sent a letter[259] to the head football coach at

[259] Kearney, A. (2021 January 21). Dedham high school fires widely respected football coach for objecting to daughter's 7th grade teacher pushing BLM propaganda and critical race theory in class. Retrieved on 2021 April 16: https://tbdailynews.com/dedham-high-school-fires-widely-respected-football-coach-for-objecting-to-daughters-

one of their high schools informing him that he would no longer be employed at the school because he objected to his 7th grade daughter being taught Critical Race Theory by her World History teacher. This coach lost his job because his employer is committed to a corrosive ideology that demeans and degrades children.

Coach Flynn found out about his termination at the same time the general public did, via a letter that reads, in part:

"We are writing today and are sorry to inform you that Dave Flynn will not be reappointed as the head coach of Dedham High School football. We met with Mr. Flynn today because he has expressed significant philosophical differences with the direction, goals and values of the school district. Due to these differences, we felt it best to seek different leadership for the program at this time."[260]

Flynn's 'philosophical differences' apparently amount to his commitment to equal treatment and equal opportunity, while his employer has abandoned that ideal in favor of the unattainable goal of equal outcomes for all.

7th-grade-teacher-pushing-blm-propaganda-and-critical-race-theory-in-class

[260] McLaughlin, T. (2021 March 3). *Brave new world of woke.* The Conway Daily Sun. Retrieved on 2021 June 8: https://www.conwaydailysun.com/opinion/columns/tom-mclaughlin-brave-new-world-of-woke/article_c0d3deee-7ba3-11eb-bf99-c79918968058.html.

Curriculum that includes these themes, which are taught within a Marxian (oppressor vs. oppressed) framework, are ubiquitous.[261] How many districts in the USA have adopted woke curriculum? The list of districts that haven't adopted it would, because it's shorter, likely be easier to gather and compile. You may be wondering how it could be that so many school districts, not to mention charter and private schools, could accept, purchase, train to, and implement ideas that are so entirely disempowering, demonizing, and subjective.

Wokeness doesn't have to be proven empirically—indeed it can't be. This accounts for at least part of its allure for would-be scholars and 'public intellectuals.' If you, as an up-and-coming scholar, don't have to expose your ideas to criticism by anyone, and if no one can double check your data for accuracy, your job becomes much easier. Of course, people are attracted to these ideas, ideologies, and theories. Who doesn't like an easy job with minimal correction or criticism?

Remember back to chapters three, four, and five where we discussed the reality-creating power of language. Curriculum in your child's school uses words in ways that you would not

---

[261] Farrow, H., (2020, July 20). The 1619 project curriculum taught in over 4,500 schools — Frederick county public schools has the option. Frederick News Post. Retrieved from: https://www.fredericknewspost.com/news/education/the-1619-project-curriculum-taught-in-over-4-500-schools-frederick-county-public-schools-has/article_a2921b75-d012-5e9e-9816-8e762539f1d4.html

recognize. We already know that 'diversity isn't what you think it is.' So, too, 'multiculturalism' and 'social emotional learning' are not what you think they are. Neither is 'character education.' To be fair, in some cases, these are terms that are used correctly—in ways that you would expect them to be used. But, because they've been abused, it behooves parents and families to carefully review materials that label themselves this way. One final example, here. 'Multiple literacies' is another way of saying 'relativism,' as Dr. Kellner explains:

"The idea behind multiple literacies is that diverse and multimodal forms of culture blend in lived experience to form new subjectivities…" (Kellner, 2003)[262]

---

[262] Kellner, D. (2003). *Toward a critical theory of education.* Democracy & Nature, *9*(1), 51-64.

Part 3: How Can We Fix It?

"Our only method of making progress on matters of controversy is to shun all forms of coercion, all the way from the subtle indoctrination of young minds to the outright physical intimidation of all."[263]

In the Spring of 2021, I received an email from a father of two children ages five and six. He asked what he could do to help them as they were being taught that the color of their skin determined whether they are good or evil—and, that they should be ashamed to be white. How would you answer this question? As I considered what I could advise this dad to do for his children, I became angry at the people who value the lives of young children so little that they would agree with and then implement curriculum that cannot do any good—even for those it purports to help. This kind of teaching can only harm them.

Parents are paying much closer attention to what their children are being taught—a silver lining that we owe, in part, to the learn-at-home virtual schooling that so many students participated in during the COVID-19 lockdowns of 2020. If you haven't already, you need to become aware of what is being

---

[263]Hicks, S.R.C., (2019). *The postmodern critique of liberal education.* Reason Papers. 41(1).

taught in your child's classroom. Ask teachers and administrators for copies of the curriculum. If you have suspicions that something is amiss, make time to get the information you need. And, if you learn that the school is inculcating their students with woke ideology, tell your friends about what you've learned and contact the teachers and principal. Try to resolve the issues there, first. If they dismiss your concerns, go to the school board. In many cases, school districts will also resist your efforts to remove this harmful material. So, you may need to consider and pursue other educational options for your kids, as mentioned in Chapter 15. School districts are supposed to be responsive to families' needs and concerns. This is what diehard government school apologists refer to as 'publicly accountable.' You and I both know that this label isn't descriptive of all school boards. In some cases, it's not even aspirational.

If you can get a large enough group of parents to support the cause for a robust and comprehensive curriculum that doesn't demonize certain groups of children based on their immutable characteristics—and disempower others—then the school board might just listen to you and alter their course. If you don't have many other education options for your children, this may be your only choice. Rest assured, effecting changes like this will not be easy or quick. You'll need all the help you can get to make it happen. But, it's possible and it's vital to the wellbeing of hundreds, if not thousands, of kids who could grow up with a healthy self-perception and commitment to mutual respect with your help.

Now that you know more about what's going on in schools across the country, you know what is happening in your child's school—or will be soon. The best thing you can do is to take the information you have and act. Act in the best interest of your child so that they, regardless of their unique characteristics, can have a happy and productive life. An education that prepares them now to interact respectfully, with compassion and caring, is one that honors the best in others; it's an education that values honest dialogue and open interpersonal communication with an understanding that every person is different. Those differences don't have to define anyone, or our relationships with them. They can (and should) add both variety and happiness to our lives.

No child, regardless of household income—or melanin—levels, should be allowed to sit in a classroom where the teacher tells them that, due to factors outside their control, they are bad. It feels inane to even have to say this, but this is the world we live in.

You've seen in the pages of this book what the ideological and philosophical bases are for the curricula used in schools throughout the Western world. Every one of them—Critical Theory, Postmodernism, Critical Pedagogy, and Critical Race Theory—reject Enlightenment values. They reject individualism in favor of essentialism. They assert that the only real thing in life is power. All of them hold up power as the primary and singular goal. It's the only thing worth having, and your goal in life should be to seek to equalize its ownership among all people at all costs.

Of course, this is all important information to have, and particularly so if you feel that something should be done about it. With the background information provided here, you should be well prepared to gather more information that is closer to your home. As you begin to get informed on how these issues are affecting your local schools, you'll be able to share with friends and neighbors. Curriculum selection processes are vital to understand, but you won't always be able to make the impact you want to, unfortunately. Your local school, school district, and elected representatives won't always be responsive to your concerns. There may come a time when you decide that your forehead just isn't going to bring down the brick wall. So, in the final chapter of Part 3, we'll discuss school choice as a possible solution. The final chapters of this book will cover some of the many ways you can learn more and then act.

Chapter 13 | Get Informed

"...there are startling examples of schools attempting to prevent parents from finding out what is being taught. For example, in Rutherford County, Tennessee, school officials asked parents to sign forms stating they would not watch their child's online classes while the district remains closed for in-person learning."[264]

The importance of understanding an issue before advocating for a particular position on it sounds like common sense, but we all fall prey to the temptation to jump into battle with a very incomplete picture of what's going on. 'Seek first to understand, then to be understood'[265] has also been expressed as 'inquiry precedes advocacy.'[266] The principle is the same. Take the time to seek out information that will help you get a clearer picture of what is really going on. To be an effective advocate for your children, you need to become informed about what is going on in their schools. Ideally, parents and advocates will dedicate an

----

[264] Butcher, J. (2020 September 10). *Some schools don't want you to know what they are teaching your kids. That's a problem.* Heritage Foundation. Retrieved on 2021 April 19: https://www.heritage.org/education/commentary/some-schools-dont-want-you-know-what-they-are-teaching-your-kids-thats-problem

[265] Covery, S.R. (1989). *The 7 habits of highly effective people.* Free Press. New York.

[266] Gerzon, M. (2006). *Leading through conflict. How successful leaders transform differences into opportunities.* Harvard Business School Press. Boston. (122).

appropriate and reasonable amount of time to understanding the issues so that we don't have to rely on low-resolution oversimplifications. We can read blogs, books, articles, and ask the people closest to our children at school, their teachers, for information about what they're actually being taught. You'll also find it helpful to gather from, and share information with others who are interested and concerned. Finally, school board meetings can help you to learn more.

Don't rely on soundbites

Well-meaning, passionate people often do harm to their causes when they choose to form their opinions on oversimplifications—soundbites. It's easy to take someone's word for explanations of concepts, definitions of words, and details of events when we don't necessarily have the time or interest to gather the information ourselves. This is why soundbites work. They act as heuristics, shortcuts to answers, when they come from people we trust or confirm what we believe to be true. Having said that, not everyone has the time to read everything ever published on these subjects. While we don't all have time to become experts on it all, we can take the time to learn enough to understand. If we do not commit to understanding to the best of our ability, within reasonable limits given our other obligations and time constraints, we run the risk of diminishing our own chances at successful advocacy. Why? People who have taken the time to understand the issue, but disagree with your position on it, will see right through you.

An example I've seen of this, on a somewhat regular basis, involves concerned parents complaining to school boards that their children are being taught Critical Race Theory. Proponents of CRT might respond with something like,

'CRT is a technique used to critique real-world systems that have negatively impacted minority populations, which are perpetuated by the oppressive majority to preserve their position of dominance. These ideas are too complex for nine-year-old children. Why would anyone even attempt to teach kids CRT? It's not happening. You don't know what you're talking about.'

This is an accurate statement, technically, but it misses the point—and I would argue that it misses the point intentionally. The concerned parent doesn't want their child to learn that they will never be able to make anything of their lives because of systemic racism—and they don't want it simply because they don't believe that oppression and failure are foregone conclusions. The parent says 'I don't want CRT taught to my child' when what they mean is 'I don't want CRT-based or CRT-aligned curricula or materials taught to my child.' Proponents of CRT will dismiss the problem by answering the statement without addressing the actual concern.

At the risk of belaboring the point, it's important to cover a little ground on this idea of the natural human tendency to believe incomplete—and therefore inaccurate—explanations of ideas, events, etc. Tversky and Kahneman (1974) published a seminal article in *Science*[267] that explains the 'how' and 'why' behind our proclivity to overestimate, favor, and underestimate and disfavor in various situations due to biases. Both proponents and opponents of the ideologies we've discussed believe that they're right, even when they know extremely little about the topic. This can be due to several different reasons, but from a cognitive psychological standpoint, the most likely culprit is availability bias. Opponents may have 'biases due to the retrievability of instances.'[268] In other words, an opponent of Postmodern ideas being used in schools might be more likely to believe a completely false account of a school in their town that is teaching children that there is no objective reality because they've seen news stories on TV lately where verified instances of such activity has occurred. This is 'availability bias.' The same goes for proponents of, say, CRT. A proponent of CRT might overestimate the number of actual discriminatory actions that minorities experience on a daily basis because they hear so much about racism and discrimination on social media, in news print, on the radio, etc. Again, this is availability bias, 'due to the

---

[267] Tversky, A., Kahneman, D. (1974). *Judgment under uncertainty: Heuristics and biases.* Science. *185*(415). 1124-1131.
[268] *Ibid.*

retrievability of instances.' Avoid the temptation to simply believe what confirms your preconceived ideas and expectations in instances that are political, yet so very personal—such as the examples given above. Having accurate information and a respectable understanding of these issues is worth the effort—and you'll be able to avoid the pitfalls mentioned.

Read, listen, and watch

There is a long and growing list of books, podcasts, blogs, and videos that cover many of the ideas in this book, though in much greater detail. I'm confident any list I could compile would be incomplete, but the titles included in *Appendix A,* at the end of this book, are not a horrible start.

You won't necessarily agree with everything you read or hear on these subjects. On some issues, you may agree wholeheartedly with an author or commentator and disagree with every other thing they say. That's okay. You're agreeing with an idea, not a person. You're disagreeing with an idea, not a person. Keeping this in mind may help you to maintain a healthy separation between people and the ideas that people spread. It's also worth remembering that ideas outlive people, which is part of the reason that eminent psychologist Carl Jung repeatedly asserted what has been popularly paraphrased as *'people don't have ideas. Ideas have people.* [269] This is most certainly the case with the ideologies discussed in this book. Unfortunately for us, people continue to perpetuate neo-Marxian Critical Theory and its philosophical offspring without considering the horrific effects of Marxism around the world during the 20th century. That these ideas have been able to survive at all, let alone thrive and gain momentum, is appalling. But, here we are. The more people know about it, however, the more likely it is to be defeated.

Ask the teachers

Despite the fact that many teachers buy into and fully support the harmful ideas that are propagated in American classrooms today (though, of course, they don't see it this way), there are still others who see that woke ideologies are at odds with their goal of empowering every child without qualification. Some teachers and administrators will be forthcoming with information about curriculum, instructional materials, lessons, and special programs. Others, unfortunately, will not. In cases that require more concerted effort, you may need to rely on official requests (usually submitted in writing) and enlisting the help of more

---

[269] This exact phrase has been attributed to Jung, and while it certainly communicates a concept that he believed, he doesn't seem to have ever used this particular phrase.

advocates to show there is support for your requests. With social media, this is easier than ever.

"The young adults who today gleefully tear down statues of the Founding Fathers were incubated in our very own schools, groomed to burst from the education system and burn America down."[270]

If you can find a teacher that wants true equality, like you do, take the opportunity to learn more about what curriculum they're teaching. Ask them about their concerns with anything they've been directed to present to students. What worksheets would they hesitate to give their own child if they were their teacher? Keep in mind while communicating with teachers in this way that they are likely putting themselves at risk by sharing anything. This may sound strange—parents should have every right to know what is being taught to their children at school—but, it's true. Even if the teacher is a member of a union, that's no guarantee that they won't be punished in some way. In fact, if teachers aren't fired outright, they can be put on administrative leave or simply prevented from interacting with students and teaching.[271]

[270] Blair, D. (2020 August 17). *I'm a former teacher. Here's how your children are getting indoctrinated by leftist ideology.* Heritage Foundation. Retrieved on 2021 June 9: https://www.heritage.org/education/commentary/im-former-teacher-heres-how-your-children-are-getting-indoctrinated-leftist.

[271] Cohen, S. (2021 April 20). *Head of NYC school that punished outspoken teacher admits school is demonizing white people.* Daily Mail. Retrieved on 2021 June 9: https://www.dailymail.co.uk/news/article-

Be sensitive to the risks, but don't stop at 'there's nothing I can do.' Families must know what their children are learning.

Join or start a parent group

As with anything, there are risks and dangers. One danger in parent groups is the tendency we all have to get upset about things that, after gathering more information, turn out to be non-issues. Put another way, sometimes we make mountains out of mole hills. This is made much easier in groups. With appropriate guards against this propensity, groups of concerned parents can be very effective in gaining information to share with one another. Another danger we all often face is that of complacency. When 'no highly visible crisis [exists],'[272] people tend to forget or deprioritize it. Try to find the proper balance between the extremes and you'll be far more effective in your efforts.

Attend school board meetings

In late 2020 and early 2021, many families around the country became more and more frustrated with district school boards

---

9491487/Head-NYC-school-punished-outspoken-teacher-admits-demonizing-white-people.html.

[272] Kotter, J. (2012). *Leading change*. Harvard Business Review Press. Boston. *41*.

over Critical Race Theory, in particular. Some districts began listening and responding[273] to this frustration, and many[274] more[275] did not.[276] Still, families continued to show up to board meetings and take the allotted three minutes per speaker to voice their opinions. Get 50 people to a school board meeting to talk about curriculum and you'll see plenty of people begin to take notice. Even in small school districts 50 parents writing emails, attending meetings, and/or calling the district office for information about curriculum, etc. is achievable. Getting angry and frustrated during public meetings is very easy given that tensions can be high and anxiety-inducing. When you're in information-gathering mode, take particular care to control your emotions and remain calm. Adding raised voices to already tense

---

[273] Nocera, J. (2021 June 20). *Chesterfield School Board joins growing backlash to critical race theory, denounces framework a year after condemning racism.* Richmond Times Dispatch. Retrieved on 2021 June 21: https://richmond.com/news/local/chesterfield-school-board-joins-growing-backlash-to-critical-race-theory-denounces-framework-a-year-after/article_31683295-c105-57bf-ad61-434d0b50cd3a.html.

[274] Taketa, K., Durham, A. (2021 June 21). *Battle over critical race theory reaches San Diego school districts.* San Diego Union-Tribune. Retrieved on 2021 June 21: https://www.sandiegouniontribune.com/news/education/story/2021-06-21/battle-over-critical-race-theory-reaches-san-diego-school-districts.

[275] Graham, J. (2021 June 17). *South Kitsap school board votes down resolution on 'critical race theory'.* Kitsap Sun. Retrieved on 2021 June 21: https://www.kitsapsun.com/story/news/2021/06/17/south-kitsap-school-board-votes-down-resolution-critical-race-theory/7729555002/.

[276] McCaughey, B. (2021 June 7). McCaughey: *School boards key in critical race theory battle.* Boston Herald. Retrieved on 2021 June 21: https://www.bostonherald.com/2021/06/07/mccaughey-school-boards-key-in-critical-race-theory-battle/.

situations rarely improves the outcome for anyone. And, given you're still seeking to understand, your chances of saying something you'll regret, or that's inaccurate, are fairly good. There's no reason, of course, that you couldn't speak during public comment period and share what you do know: that you're gathering information because you sincerely care about your child and the children in your community; that you'll research and share what you learn with other parents to ensure they're as informed as possible. These are things you can express respectfully and honestly to the elected members of the school board. You may even decide that you want to run for election to your school board precisely so that you can increase transparency for families. Your community would be better off for it, as well. If you're not interested in running for election yourself, you may consider working with the current school board members to make instructional materials more available to parents.

You can be a great help to currently-serving board members. Many of them are blinded to the seriousness of these issues because they're too used to them—like a fish doesn't notice the water it lives in. For kids—who only have one shot at their early education—this type of 'insider myopia can be deadly.'[277] Do your research on each board member. Learn about them, their

---

[277] Kotter, J. (2012). *Leading change.* Harvard Business Review Press. Boston. *52.*

experience and backgrounds. Ask friends and neighbors if they know any of them personally. Getting to know the members of the board better will help you prepare more effectively to interact with them on these important issues. Your preparation ahead of time will vastly increase your comfort level when you begin to engage and take action.

Chapter 14 | Get Involved

"Parents, the longer that you wait and you don't hold your child's schools accountable, gives these guys more time to dictate what's best for your child's physical, mental, and emotional health. Don't be afraid to speak out for your kids because they are voiceless and they rely on you. Students...do not allow anybody to tell you that you cannot accomplish anything because of your skin color, or to hate yourself because of your skin color. Students, it is up to you to become the next generation of victims, or victors."[278]

What is your goal?

This is a vital question to ask yourself as you begin to consider ways to take action. If you gather up a bunch of information and you recognize that there is a lot of deeply harmful material that shouldn't have any place in schools, and then simply become angry and resentful, you're not going to be very effective in making changes that can ameliorate the problem. You need to decide what it is that you want to achieve as a result of what you know. Because I value individual liberty so highly, I am most

---

[278] Vanetsyan, L. (2021 June 8). *Loudoun County School Board Meeting.* [Video]. Retrieved on 2021 June 8: http://go.boarddocs.com/vsba/loudoun/Board.nsf/goto?open&id=C3 DHGM4869B4.

likely to favor efforts that achieve the maximization of that particular measure. I've been fortunate to have opportunities to do just that. I work to expand school choice options for students and families on a daily basis. In some places, this is easier than in others. But, every town, city, county, prefect, state, province, and country has room to improve. I don't know of one country that couldn't make adjustments to their education statutes and systems in ways that would increase student choice, achievement, and attainment. We'll discuss this specifically in Chapter 16.

You can choose to strike out on your own, or join a group of likeminded people who have similar goals in mind. If there are already groups formed and communicating on a regular basis about these issues, all the better. You may need to start spreading the word and gathering a group of people if there isn't something already in place. Ask five friends to join you and get them to ask five friends as well. Before long, you'll have a group big enough to get attention on these important issues.

Families and parents need to get involved in ways that allow their voices to be heard. For some, this will mean recording video conversations about upcoming board meetings or curriculum programs. Others may be more comfortable writing an op-ed for the local newspaper or blog. I've met many people who truly want to support efforts they care about, but the limelight isn't for them. They've found fulfillment in simply helping others to accomplish their roles through graphic design, handing out flyers, or managing a contact list. Everyone can contribute in a way that is helpful. Working in groups with diverse abilities is an effective and rewarding experience.

State legislators are always on the lookout for concerned families who will take the time to testify at a hearing for a bill. This is a great way to get involved and it's not difficult. A phone call or email to your legislators will connect you with influential people who could use your help in a common cause—even if you don't happen to agree on every issue.

Having difficult conversations

You are going to have rough conversations. Not necessarily because you can't express yourself well, or because the other person is combative, but because you are raising serious concerns about the teaching of children. You're not disagreeing about the best kind of cheese (which is Swiss, of course), you're disagreeing about something that someone else believes themselves to be expert in. There are some helpful tips to keep in mind as you set out to share your opinion and preferences with people who won't always agree with you.

"...express what you see and why you see it that way, how you feel and maybe who you are. Self-knowledge and the belief that what you want to share is important will take you significantly further than eloquence and wit."[279]

Your goal shouldn't necessarily be to convince everyone else that what you want for your child is also what they should want for their children or the students they are expected to serve. This expectation will be met regularly with disappointment. No doubt you'll find others who agree wholeheartedly with your positions. But, you can't hope to gain the support of everyone. Be that as it may, remaining silent is not a viable option, as Audre Lourde wisely and eloquently pointed out:

"I have come to believe...that what is most important to me must be spoken, made verbal and shared, even at the risk of having it bruised or misunderstood."

"...what I most regretted were my silences..."

"Your silence will not protect you..."

"...we have been socialized to respect fear more than our own needs for language and definition, and while we wait in silence for that final luxury of fearlessness, the weight of that silence will choke us."[280]

---

[279] Stone, D., Patton, B., Heen, S. (1999). *Difficult conversations: How to discuss what matters most.* Viking. New York. *185.*

[280] Lourde, A. (2007). *Sister outsider: Essays and speeches.* Penguin Random House. New York.

Social Media

Time spent on social media platforms can range from wasteful to painful—and sometimes helpful and informative. You can help by sharing your experiences and encouraging friends and neighbors to do the same. The power of social media has been demonstrated time and time again. We've all seen some of the most powerful organizations in the world respond (and quickly) to large groups of ordinary people on social media platforms. If you can manage to find enough like-minded people who are willing to work with you to share important information in an effort to protect children, you might be surprised at the amount of influence you can have. There are already a lot of powerful and influential voices on various platforms that you can connect with, learn from, and potentially collaborate with.

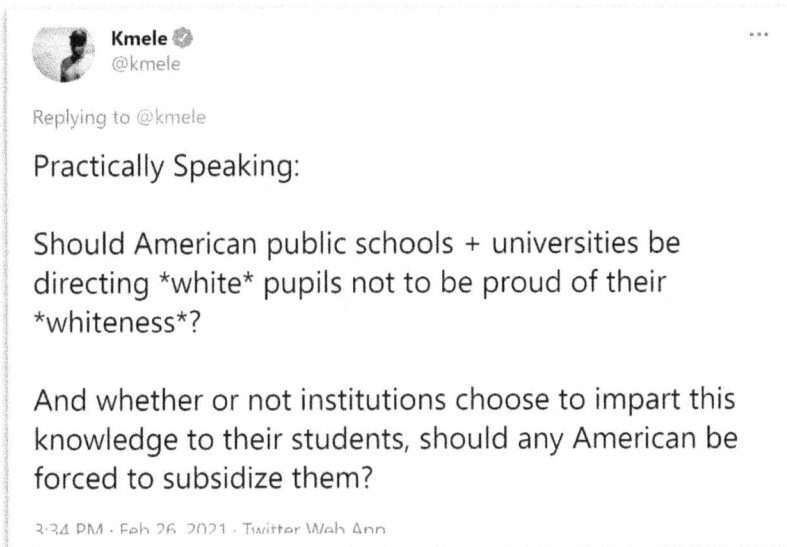

Kmele ✓
@kmele

Replying to @kmele

Practically Speaking:

Should American public schools + universities be directing *white* pupils not to be proud of their *whiteness*?

And whether or not institutions choose to impart this knowledge to their students, should any American be forced to subsidize them?

3:34 PM · Feb 26 2021 · Twitter Web App

Working with teachers

The first thing to remember and carefully consider is that teachers are employees. To the extent that they deliver material they don't personally believe in, they're almost certainly being required to do so by their employer. The opposite can also be true. Some teachers may be forbidden from teaching specific concepts or material and still do it anyway because they believe in it so much that the risk is worth it to them. You may not know whether your child's teacher is in one of these positions or in another altogether, namely, they don't have particularly strong feelings one way or another about the curriculum and they're simply doing as they're told. Once you find out, you can engage the teacher by courteously asking questions about how they feel about diversity, equity, CRT, and liberative education to better understand the situation. You might consider sharing resources you've pulled together in your study of these topics. Teachers, like the rest of us, lead busy lives and may have never been exposed to viewpoints that oppose those they're being required to teach your child. Assuming they know everything you do and that they're maliciously attempting to bring about a communist revolution by indoctrinating your child could be just slightly overboard. Consider carefully the attitude you take into your conversations with the teacher. It may well be that they are consciously training revolutionaries.[281] Best not to start with that presumption, however.

Working with administrators

The further away you get from the teacher, the more difficult resolution becomes. The teacher has near-absolute control over what happens in their classrooms, and this is particularly the case in district schools where administrative control is relatively less stringent than in private or charter schools—generally speaking. Sometimes, however, your efforts to seek resolution with the teacher will fail and taking the conversation to school administration will be necessary. Principals and vice principals are your next-best option. As mentioned previously, you may find that administrators don't want to engage with you on the philosophies that are taught to children through the curriculum they're implementing. There could be any number of specific reasons for this, but the majority of those boil down to just a few primary excuses. First, they may be very uncomfortable with conflict and choose to avoid it at all costs—including ignoring you. Next, they may disagree with you because they actually feel that CRT, CT, PM, and CP are beneficial to young children.

---

[281] Dougherty, J. (2021 May 25). *Portland teachers exposed for radicalizing students, training them to become 'revolutionaries'*. Retrieved on 2021 June 24: https://indeki.com/portland-teachers-exposed-for-radicalizing-students-training-them-to-become-revolutionaries.html.

Last, they might just be 'too busy.' Remember that when people consistently choose not to set and keep appointments with you to discuss controversial curricula they're teaching in schools, they're consciously avoiding you.

'I don't care how busy you are, if you can't make time for the people who need you, then you're not really busy, you're just disorganized,'[282] and I'll add, *'or you could be a pusillanimous ideologue.'*

It may be that you do get an administrator to talk with you, and they may even give you assurances that your perspective is valued—and then they do exactly the opposite of what you agreed.

In North Carolina, a group of concerned citizens formed an organization that informs families about what is going on in their children's schools, among other things. They published a web page devoted to awareness about surveys that children were being forced to complete in school. These surveys gathered information about kids' gender, sexuality, home life, and other personal information that is linked to each student's ID number. One parent called her child's principal and requested that her student be opted out of the survey. The following day, the

---

[282] McCormack, M.H. (1998). *On communicating.* Dove Books. Los Angeles. *48.*

principal coerced the child to complete the survey.[283] While there are most certainly plenty of school administrators that would do exactly what this principal did, there are also many that would honor the wishes of the parent.

The moral: learn, understand, speak up, and then *stay awake*.

Working with school districts

"I have a lot of questions. I'm asking them. I wish that my questions would have been answered without having to do it this way. But they told me to do it with their own questions. They're teaching something that they're trying to hide from you."[284]

When you're ready to start engaging with your school district, remember to 'never underestimate the magnitude of the forces that reinforce complacency and that help maintain the status quo.'[285] This is no truer than in school districts run by the

[283] EFA. (n.d.). *Stop North Carolina's child spying program.* Education First Alliance. Retrieved on 2021 June 24: https://www.edfirstnc.org/petition.

[284] Nelson, J.Q. (2021 June 2). *RI mom says she could face lawsuit after demanding answers on CRT curriculum in elementary school.* Fox News. Retrieved on 2021 June 24: https://www.foxnews.com/media/rhode-island-mother-lawsuit-critical-race-theory-requests.

[285] Kotter, J. (2012). *44.*

government. Your job, then, is to 'force discussion of honest information at meetings...'[286]

Working with the state

> *"Education reform is not important to your government unless it's important to the head of your government—personally."*[287]

Elected officials tend to respond to organized constituencies. There's a good reason for this, even though it can be very easy to be cynical about their lack of attention to 'the common people.' Politicians hear from a lot of people, all the time. If they hear the *same thing* from *a lot of people, all the time*, then they know they have more than 'one-off' aberrations...coincidences. Keep in mind that when you're dealing with the state, whether that's elected legislators and officials, or employees of government agencies, you're dealing with other humans. Many of us have a natural tendency to hold people with certain titles up and assign additional value or weight to their statements and opinions. Yes, their perspectives can result in consequential outcomes in policy and law. There's no doubt about that. There's also no doubt about the reality that they're still just people.

---

[286] Kotter, J. (2012). *45.*
[287] Fullan, M. (2011). *Change leader: Learning to do what matters most.* Jossey Bass. San Francisco. *39.*

"My views and feelings are as legitimate, valuable, and important as yours—no more, but no less."[288]

You've heard many people speak who had limited vocabularies and education but were still capable of delivering powerful statements. They had at least a few things going for them. What they have to say is *relevant* and they *understand* what they're talking about. They 'do not go around making random assertions.'[289]

"As you embark on a difficult conversation, ask yourself, 'Have I said what is at the heart of the matter for me? Have I shared what is at stake?' If not, ask yourself why, and see if you can find the courage to try."[290]

To reiterate, the more proximity you can maintain by involving those closest to the issue, the more likely you are to find success, since implementation is accomplished by the people 'on the ground.' Working with the state should be a last resort and, ideally, any action by the state would result in increased options and freedom, not a decrease.

---

[288] Stone, D., Patton, B., Heen, S. (1999). *186.*
[289] Fullan, M. (2011). *Change leader: Learning to do what matters most.* Jossey Bass. San Francisco. *81.*
[290] Stone, D., Patton, B., Heen, S. (1999). *191.*

Chapter 15 | Curriculum Selection

"...institutional, structural, and systemic racism ha[ve] been engrained in the history of America and throughout its public education system. [NSBA] is dedicated to understanding and recognizing the root causes of barriers to equitable educational outcomes for each child."[291]

What can be done?

There is some variance in who is authorized to purchase and implement curriculum. In most school districts, school boards, and even principals, can make those decisions. The same is true of independent charter schools and private schools. Families ought to have some power and voice in the process of curriculum adoption. In school districts, elected school boards should be actively engaging parents to be sure everyone is heard, and treated as constituents they represent—which they are. In schools of choice (charter, private and micro-schools), parents have more flexibility to 'vote with their feet' by moving to a school that best meets their needs and expectations. 'Generating short-term

---

[291] DIRE. (n.d.). DIRE: Dismantling institutional racism in education. Retrieved on: 2021 April 19. https://www.nsba.org/Advocacy/Equity/DIRE. National School Boards Association.

wins'[292] is a powerful way to build momentum around your local movement to return decision-making power in K-12 curriculum to the hands of families. You might do this by meeting with select school board members, informally, with a small group to discuss concerns and suggestions. Another short-term win might be getting a vote or two on the school board in favor of empowering all children to learn and develop, rather than disempowering and demonizing groups of kids in school. Ultimately, the goal will be to ensure children and families have control over their education, that their education is of sufficient quality to prepare them for a happy and productive life, and that all of this happens for every child regardless of how they look or how much money their parents make.

How is curriculum adopted?

There are at least *five different paths* that curriculum can take into a public school classroom. The remainder of this chapter will walk through each of the five most common ways this happens in schools. There is wide variation in actual adoption processes for educational materials in large part because adoption can occur both formally and informally. Some individuals in K-12 education will simply do what they want without following any prescribed process. Further, many parents

---

[292] Kotter, J. (2012).

have been surprised to find that new materials, new procedures, and new initiatives are instituted without notification to parents or district administrators. Often this is made possible by labeling them 'pilot programs.' Yes, principals can commonly implement school-wide changes without any kind of approval, per se, by claiming it's a 'pilot program.' But, your child's teacher can introduce material to their students without even the hassle of such a label.

The teacher

The *first* is the most common: the teacher. Teachers in many schools have at least some flexibility in what and how they present certain topics to their students. Certainly, there are state standards that must be addressed in preparation for end-of-grade exams and so forth. But, the reality is that not every one of the approximately 1,000+ hours is spent only on topics that will be on the state test at the end of the year. Instruction time can be used very differently by one teacher than another—even within the same school. Private schools and charter schools have the ability to be more prescriptive with curriculum—and demand fidelity to that curriculum—than district schools.

A 1990-1991 survey of public and private school principals asked which groups had a 'great deal' of influence over curriculum choices.[293] They ranked teachers above themselves. We should note here that respondents to the survey may have considered the question as pertaining only to official decisions about curriculum. Otherwise, teachers likely would have even had a much higher total.

The principal

The *second* most common way curriculum is adopted at a school is by the principal. School leaders are given a certain amount of autonomy as to how they'll use their budgets for textbooks, workbooks, professional development, etc.

To the extent that principals have influence over curriculum choices, parents must make their wishes concerning the education of their children known so that alignment can be achieved. A natural question arises as we discuss who can influence what our children are taught: 'who influences the influencers?' The National Association of Elementary School Principals (NAESP) has over 15,000 member principals from elementary and middle/junior high schools. On the organization's website home page, they provide a link to an event held on April 28, 2021 titled, *'What Principals Need to*

---

[293] NCES. (1995). *Who influences decisionmaking about school curriculum: What do principals say?* U.S. Department of Education. National Center for Education Statistics. Retrieved on 2021 March 8: https://nces.ed.gov/pubs95/95780.pdf.

Know About Implicit Racial Bias.'[294] Dr. Sylvia Perry of Project Implicit was the featured presenter at the event. Her organization uses the Implicit Association Test, or IAT, according to their website. The IAT is much more widely used than its accuracy or usefulness warrants. Even the people who created it have made a point to publicly state that its results should not be taken too seriously—that is, after they said that the test was important and accurate. Well, it should be noted, also, that they then backtracked and said again that the test is very valuable and can predict behavior. So, what we've got so far from the creators of the IAT is that the test is both worthwhile, and not, and both accurate, and not. Where does this leave us? If we look to others' opinions of the test, there are plenty of reasons to doubt the IAT is anything more than a fancy mood ring[295]—the kind of mood ring that has an entire business built around it that charges organizations thousands and tens of thousands of dollars to convince employees that this computer-based test that you can take in the comfort of your own home will reveal the extent to which you are a racist. This is just one example of the kind of 'services' and training content that NAESP is providing to its

---

[294] NAESP. (2021). What principals need to know about implicit racial bias. NAESP. Retrieved on 2021 June 5: https://www.naesp.org/event/what-principals-need-to-know-about-implicit-racial-bias/

[295] Singal, J. (2017 December 5). *The creators of the Implicit Association Test should get their story straight.* New York Magazine. Retrieved on 2021 June 5: https://nymag.com/intelligencer/2017/12/iat-behavior-problem.html.

members. The NAESP counts somewhere between 10% and 20% of principals in the U.S. among its members. What about the other 80%-90%? The National Education Association (NEA) and American Federation of Teachers (AFT) together have millions and millions of teachers, administrators, and staff in their membership. Just in case you thought any significant portion of educators in American school weren't affected by this, both NEA[296] and AFT[297] provide links to the same organization (Project Implicit) where the test can be taken. Talk about implicit bias, microaggressions, diversity, inclusion, equity, and racism is constant in these organizations. Teachers are being trained on these topics nonstop.

School districts across the country have been under an increasingly scrutinous microscope in recent years due to revelations about rampant misspending,[298] horrific abuse of schoolchildren,[299] and the introduction of divisive curricula.[300]

[296] NEA. (n.d.). *Implicit bias, microaggressions, and stereotype resources.* National Education Association. Retrieved on 2021 June 5: https://www.nea.org/resource-library/implicit-bias-microaggressions-and-stereotypes-resources.

[297] AFT. (2015). Understanding implicit bias. American Educator.

[298] Butcher, J.M. (2020 May 19). *Bad education: Why shocking public school corruption remains hidden.* Heritage Foundation. Retrieved on 2021 June 5: https://www.heritage.org/education/commentary/bad-education-why-shocking-public-school-corruption-remains-hidden.

[299] Choice Media. (n.d.). *Sexual abuse in schools.* Choice Media. Retrieved on 2021 June 5: SexualAbuseInSchools.org

[300] What Are They Learning?. (n.d.). *What are they learning?* Retrieved on 2021 June 5: http://whataretheylearning.com.

The school district

Third, these districts have the authority to dictate to their schools what, how, and when they teach children, within the boundaries of state and federal laws. School district boards in the United States consist of elected officials who are meant to represent the interests of their constituents relative to their local government-funded schools. They provide guidance and direction to district administrators who are then responsible to carry out the decisions of the board. One of the duties of the district superintendent is to make curriculum recommendations for consideration by the board. Often, these recommendations don't get much of a public hearing because they are included as items on the consent agenda of a board meeting, which don't require public discussion. Sometimes new programs will be explained in the public meeting of the board, which may be the only time parents hear about new instructional materials—for the parents who take the time to pay attention to those meetings.

The state bureaucracy

State departments of education have the power to direct publicly-funded schools (subject to the limitations in state statutes) on matters of curriculum content. This is the *fourth* path that new content can take into a school. Generally speaking, most states leave specific curriculum selections in the hands of teachers, principals, and districts. However, it is not uncommon for state departments of education (SDE) to specify particular requirements be met. As the administrative arm of the state in all matters of K-12 education, they have responsibility to create and communicate learning standards for all publicly-funded schools. It is these standards that parents need to be aware of and research so that they understand exactly what is being required of K-12 teachers. For decades, SDEs have added more and more standards that must be accomplished by teachers. Those standards have included an increasing number of requirements that are based on CRT, CT, CP, and PM. With the widespread adoption of Common Core starting in the late 2000's, many states shared similar requirements as to what children should learn prior to high school graduation. While many states proudly proclaimed they had shunned Common Core in favor of state-specific standards, even they still largely mirror the rest of the country—with some minor modifications here and there.

In addition to SDEs, state boards of education influence (and provide various levels of governance over) local school districts. NSBA is the nationwide association for school boards that enroll over two thirds of all K-12 students in the country. The National School Boards Association (NSBA) "...*is a federation of state associations and the U.S. territory of the Virgin Islands that represent locally elected school board officials serving approximately 51 million public school students*..." There are a little over 76 million school-aged children in the U.S. This group trains and advises state-level school board association members on everything from governance and policy to purchasing and advocacy. NSBA mentions 'equity' scores of times on their website and even held an online equity symposium for members in February 2021 with over 2,000 attendees. State boards of education also belong to the National Association of State Boards of Education, whose website includes a strong emphasis on 'equity.' The popularity of this word spread so quickly through organizations over the past few years that one is made to wonder whether many of the people using the word, including those serving on state boards of education, actually understand what it means. It is entirely possible that most state bureaucrats are unwittingly promoting 'equity' because they believe it means the same thing as equality. However, there are plenty of people who know exactly what it means as well as the incongruence between its popular definition and how it manifests in practice.

The legislature

The *fifth* way that curriculum can make it into your child's classroom is through your state's legislature. Lawmakers can dictate that a certain concept be taught, or conversely, banned in public schools. Rarely do legislatures become very prescriptive in the specifics of education operations or academics. It is duplicative and redundant for them to make a habit of involving themselves in decisions like this. Involvement at this level also forfeits the benefits of proximity: the closest entity to the issue at hand is best positioned to address it.

While each of these five ways can be used to get ideas in front of your children at school, as noted, some are used much more frequently than others. The most common method of introducing different materials to a child is via the teacher.

The best way?

A final method of curriculum selection is worth mentioning, even though it is not as common as the five listed above. I mention it here with the hope that you might be able to work with your school to implement it. Some school districts have formed 'curriculum selection committees' which sometimes include parents as members. There are at least two very significant benefits to forming such a committee. First, as a parent representative, you will have inside knowledge of the curriculum that is under consideration at all times. You can then share what you know with other parents to ensure transparency—a perfectly reasonable expectation. You might choose to share this information with other parents in a parent group on social media, through an email newsletter, or at regular in-person meetings. Each of these are great ways to build community around the shared interest of your children's education.

The second benefit of participating in such a committee is that you will be able to influence decisions that affect your children and your neighbors' children. This can be a very difficult, but also immensely rewarding role. Having said that, there should be no doubt that a curriculum selection committee won't necessarily have power over all curriculum. However, any influence is more than parents have right now in most schools in America. So, while we work for more, we do the best we can with what we have. Parents who care about what their children are being taught will, over the next several years, be working with legislators to increase parental influence on curriculum selection and expand school choice opportunities for children.

Chapter 16 | School choice

The year 2020 was what we might call a "Great Awakening in Education." Parents of the more than 70 million students in America got a much clearer picture of what is being taught in their children's classrooms. Some of it turned out to be very good, and some not so good. Teachers allowing students to bully their classmates during virtual class sessions, indoctrinating kids with unproven and controversial curriculum, and in some cases even mistreating and berating students themselves.

Allowing families to select the type of education their children receive is, aside from being the right thing to do, the only way to preserve equality of opportunity while respecting the freedom of each individual. In principle, educational freedom is the only viable option. Unfortunately, elected officials don't often operate on principle—as evidenced by their stunning hypocritical

---

[301] Shanker, A. (former United Federation of Teachers President) quoted in Klein, J. (2011 May 10). *Scenes from the New York education wars.* Wall Street Journal.

opposition to school choice generally.[302] As a result, we have a largely monopolistic public education system in America, while several countries around the globe enjoy a plethora of options for their children's schooling. We can do better by our students than we are—via school choice—and there's plenty of reason to do so even for our neighbors who aren't very concerned about ideology in their children's classrooms. On that note, many families may want CRT taught in their children's classrooms. They may be ardent supporters of these ideologies. More power to them. Let them find a school that teaches their children the way they see fit—just don't force everyone else's kids into the same religion. We can advocate for extension to our neighbors the same freedoms we want relative to our children's education. Where school choice isn't currently available to all students, the only recourse families have is to ensure that schools aren't undoing the work that parents who value Enlightenment principles are doing at home.

A common critique of school choice, whether charter schools, vouchers, or tuition tax credits, is that underprivileged students and families are harmed by policies that increase educational options. Of course, affluent families are well-positioned to select a district or private school. But, giving those options to families who don't have the resources to pay directly for them is

---

[302] EFI. (n.d.). *School choice hypocrisy map.* Educational Freedom Institute. Retrieved on 2021 April 21: http://efinstitute.org/school-choice-hypocrisy-map/.

'irresponsible.' Put another way, 'poor people can't make good decisions about education.' Aside from being bigoted and elitist, it's also a thinly-veiled argument for increasing power over families by limiting their freedom to choose.[303] Ideologues who buy into this narrative see themselves as benevolent caregivers. When, in practice, they are paternalistic authoritarians.

K-12 education in America includes a wide variety of options for families—if you happen to be wealthy, or if you live in one of the few states where that variety is made available to low-income students. Unfortunately for students, even where many education options are available to them, the teachers who instruct them will have found it extremely difficult to escape indoctrination during their time in university.

Due to the influence and power of monied teacher unions, America's public schooling system is particularly vulnerable to mass adoption of philosophies, practices, and even specific curricula.

Choice gives parents control over education

It's about time that parents gained control over what their children are learning; they're their children, after all. Choice

---

[303] DeAngelis, C.A., McCluskey, N.P., (2020). *School choice myths.* Cato Institute. Washington, D.C. (177).

gives parents and students alike a sense of ownership that simply cannot be replicated in compulsory systems, certainly not at the same scale. In the United States, regardless of where you live, you are able to select the food you eat from many different grocery stores. You can choose which gas stations and convenience stores you'll patronize. You can even choose which providers educate your children—but only if they're not in Kindergarten through the twelfth grades. Taxpayer-funded preschool programs allow parents to take money to virtually any preschool provider. Taxpayer-funded university programs allow students to take money to virtually any college or university. But, if your student is between those two groups in age, you must live in one of the few states that has a variety of school choice programs available to families—states like Arizona and Florida—in order to have anywhere near the same flexibility.

This inconsistency should not be chalked up to misfortune or written off as insurmountable. Parents are best positioned to make choices for their children, and there is some good news in this regard. State legislatures around the country advanced and passed numerous school choice bills in the sessions that began in early 2021. Now, in more states than ever, students can access education options that match most closely their needs—rather than being forced to attend the school they live closest to, as if physical proximity is the appropriate determinant in education providers.

It is hard for me to understand what harm is going to be done by allowing parents to have a choice as compared to having self-interested bureaucrats have a monopoly.[304]

Reductions in Crime

It stands to reason that students who have a choice of where to attend school will be less likely to have behavior problems. This is not meant to suggest that all crime will disappear, of course. Over the past 5-10 years, more and more research has been done on the positive effects of school choice on students, and the impact they can have on their communities. Students who are given a choice of where to attend school tend to commit fewer crimes as youth[305] and as adults.[306]

"...students in the [private school choice] program were 53% less likely to commit drug crimes and 86% less likely to commit property crimes than peers in public schools. Private schools can enforce discipline and teach moral values without fear of political complications."[307]

---

[304] Sowell, T., Buckley, W.F., (1981, November 12). The Economic Lot of Minorities [TV series episode]. In *Firing Line with William F. Buckley*. Stanford University.

[305] DeAngelis, C.A.; Wolf, P.J. (2020). *Private school choice and character: More evidence from Milwaukee.* The Journal of Private Enterprise, 35 (3).

[306] DeAngelis, C.A. (2019). *Private school choice and crime: Evidence from Milwaukee.* Social Science Quarterly. 100 (6). https://doi.org/10.1111/ssqu.12698

[307] Editorial Board. (2020 August 30). *The year of school choice.* Wall Street Journal.

While it may not be as simple as having a choice—certainly, a choice that best meets the needs of a student would be ideal—we can be confident that families prefer the opportunity to select how and where their children are educated. While there are risks to allowing everyone to choose what their kids learn in school via school choice, could they really do any more damage than government-run schools are doing now?

Increased safety

Safety at school is a growing concern for families. News reports of violence and fighting, in addition to tragic school shootings, seem to be increasing in frequency over time. Every instance causes parents to think twice about the environment they're sending their children into on a daily basis. There are hundreds of thousands of these families that have found a better way to address those concerns than to simply hope no harm comes to their kids: school choice. Families who are able to choose their schools are likely to make their selection based on safety, and their choices often produce the expected outcome[308]—their children are safer at school.[309]

Increased innovation

Some relevant research seems to "...suggest that the adoption of compulsory schooling in the United States reduced patents per capita and output per worker over time."[310] With so few options available to the majority of America's 76 million school-aged children, compelling them to go to their local district school may actually be harming them, and our society—or, at the very least, holding them back from what they could accomplish if they were freed to choose. There is no doubt that a one-size-fits-all solution for the education of K-12 students in America is unlikely to meet the individual needs of so many children. That goes without saying. But, the question of innovation is an interesting one that, if students had open access to a variety of school options, may be increased and improved—with the whole of society positioned to

---

[308] DeAngelis, C., Lueken, M., (2019). *School sector and climate: An analysis of K-12 safety policies and school climates in Indiana.* Social Science Quarterly. 101(1).

[309] Schwalbach, J., (2020). *School choice lets parents pick safer schools.* Heritage Foundation. https://www.heritage.org/education/commentary/school-choice-lets-parents-pick-safer-schools

[310] DeAngelis, C., Dills, A. (2020). Does compulsory schooling affect innovation? Evidence from the United States. Social Science Quarterly. 101 (5) 1728-1742. https://doi.org/10.1111/ssqu.12832

benefit. As Wagner and Dintersmith note, what's needed most today and in the future is critical thinking skills[311]—the primary ingredient of innovation. Kids sitting passively in a classroom all for 180 days each year and completing multiple choice tests hardly seems the ideal circumstance to produce minds that can innovate.

There is every reason to take the decision-making power for the education of children away from government and give it to families. Students do not belong to government, and they certainly don't belong to a particular school. Some education reform advocates have been criticized by other prominent pro-school choice individuals over their rejection of woke ideologies' propagation within the district school systems in the United States. Their concern seems to be that the intensity of the debate over classroom content could not only distract from the goal of individual choice in education, but that it could actually result in a schism that threatens the effectiveness of the movement as a whole. 'We worked so hard to get all these voices working in unison and now some peoples' opposition to CRT in classrooms threatens to spoil the whole thing!' There are a couple of important items to keep in mind on this note. First, arguments over curriculum aren't likely to pull the rug out from under charter schools, vouchers, tuition tax credits, etc. There are

---

[311] Wagner, T., Dintersmith, T. (2015) *Most likely to succeed.* Scribner. New York. 224.

simply too many parents whose eyes have been opened up to the disappointing reality that comprises government-run schools.[312] The lockdowns of 2020 made sure of that.[313] There has never been more support for school choice. Second, why does it make any sense to allow your child to sit in a classroom for seven hours each day where they're told they're either evil or incapable, when you could simultaneously be working for more school options and less indoctrination in class? Parents can 'walk and chew gum,' as the saying goes. Having said that, in most states where charter school laws have been passed, the process to open a new charter school can take up to four years—if everything goes smoothly. If things don't go smoothly, you may be doomed to a repeat of the complete disallowance of charter schools as in Danbury, CT, a drought that lasted for 22 years after the state passed a law allowing charter schools. These delays were caused by the 'existing educational establishment.'[314]

Teacher unions and their allies have been successfully stigmatizing school choice advocates and programs for decades—since their inception. They want complete control over

---

[312] See *SchoolChoicePolling.com*

[313] Butcher, J., Burke, L. (2021 February 9). *The education lesson from COVID lockdowns: School choice is imperative for every child.* Heritage Foundation. Retrieved on 2021 June 7: https://www.heritage.org/education/commentary/the-education-lesson-covid-lockdowns-school-choice-imperative-every-child.

[314] Sowell, T. (2020). *Charter schools and their enemies.* Basic Books. New York. *65.*

education for at least two reasons. First, they believe that they know what is best for your child. Second, they want all people who work in the field of education to be unionized. Full unionization means a constant flow of large amounts of union dues to pay their leadership. Most charter schools and private schools are not unionized. As a result, teacher unions don't like or support charter or private schools. Worse still, they fight against any form of school choice that doesn't also support their near-monopoly on American K-12 education. Once you recognize this is the status quo, their statements and positions on school choice, espoused by their representatives, spokespeople, and members make much more sense. All of their 'principled opposition' to charter schools, vouchers, or tuition tax credits is suspect. Do they really believe that vouchers are inherently bad, or do they just see clearly the threat they pose to their stranglehold on the classroom?

Families across America need to find ways to advocate for school choice. Without this, we're doomed to continue the cycle of reactive attempts to control our neighbors and vice versa. It is true that some things must be enshrined in law. Those things generally should be limited to protections against infringements on personal liberty. The ideal protection for freedom in K-12 education is absolute school choice. You get what you want and so does your neighbor. This should be our shared goal.

Conclusion

America is over 100 years into an experiment in K-12 education that has the vast majority of kids attending schools that are run by government. That experiment is largely failing. To the extent that it's working at all, it's working only for students who enjoy enough support outside the classroom to supplement in-class instruction. Funding isn't the issue. Even if it was a problem, the data does not support the notion that more money equates to better outcomes for students.[315] Further, experience has taught us that when government allocates more money to K-12 education, rarely does the money increase the salaries of teachers[316]—a move that is likely to attract more and better teacher candidates. Why wouldn't unions want to increase the pay of teachers? Because increasing the number of dues-paying staff is a much more lucrative option for the union. The explosive growth of 'all other staff' on school campuses is direct evidence of this strategy by the unions. It's perfectly reasonable that an organization would implement strategies that are designed to help them grow, or at least perpetuate their existence. Why wouldn't the teachers unions prioritize their own survival? Next time the unions feign

---

[315] Flanders, W. (2018 August 29). *Spending more money on schools doesn't help students learn.* Washington Examiner. Retrieved on 2021 June 9: https://www.washingtonexaminer.com/opinion/spending-more-money-on-schools-doesnt-help-students-learn.

[316] Scafidi, B. (2017). *Back to the staffing surge: The great teacher salary stagnation and the decades-long employment growth in American public schools.* EdChoice. Retrieved on 2021 June 9: https://eric.ed.gov/?id=ED583004.

concern for students above all else, remember what they're advocating for through their lobbyists and teaching your children in the schools they run.

In the meantime, we need to find ways to remind everyone whose children are being taught harmful ideologies in what many, until recently, believed to be safe and caring environments. Students do not belong to any school, whether district, private, or charter. There are too many schools in each of these sectors that are teaching children that 'all that matters is power,' that they are 'oppressed or oppressors,' and that the only way out of the 'horrors of modern life' is to burn down capitalism so that everyone can 'be equal.' They're training kids to essentialize their friends based solely on their melanin levels. These ideas are in widely-used curriculum. They're in elementary education courses at universities throughout the Western world. They are in professional development workshops for teachers and administrators at your local school.

Appendix A | Suggested Books, Podcasts, Websites, and Blogs

The following lists are presented in no particular order. Each of them have helped me to better understand the ideas discussed in this book. These lists are incomplete. There are hundreds and hundreds of titles that could and should accompany a comprehensive survey of the material. For the sake of space, the lists are kept to a manageable number. Lastly, I have not included academic papers/articles in this list. To truly understand the scope of the issues discussed in this book, readers would do well to read journal articles, as well.

Suggested Books
- *Explaining Postmodernism* (Dr. Stephen Hicks)
- *Losing the Race* (Dr. John McWhorter)
- *The Content of Our Character* (Dr. Shelby Steele)
- *Discrimination and Disparities* (Dr. Thomas Sowell)
- *Cynical Theories* (Helen Pluckrose & Dr. James Lindsay)
- *Self-portrait in Black & White* (Thomas Chatterton Williams)
- *Toxic Diversity* (Dr. Dan Subotnik)
- *Please Stop Helping Us* (Jason Riley)
- *Cultural Literacy* (E.D. Hirsch)

Suggested Podcasts
- *The Glenn Show* (Glenn Loury & John McWhorter)
- *Open College* (Dr. Stephen Hicks)
- *The Dark Horse* (Dr. Bret Weinstein)
- *Honestly with Bari Weiss* (Bari Weiss)
- *Conversations with Coleman* (Coleman Hughes)

Suggested Websites/Blogs
- *Quillette.com*
- *NewDiscourses.com*
- *Plato.Stanford.edu*